New Daylight

Edited by **Sally Welch** September–December 2021

The Bible Reading Fellowship
15 The Chambers, Vineyard
Abingdon OX14 3FE
brf.org.uk

The Bible Reading Fellowship (BRF) is a Registered Charity (233280)

ISBN 978 1 80039 034 8
All rights reserved

This edition © The Bible Reading Fellowship 2021
Cover image: Glendalough Valley, Wicklow Mountains National Park, Ireland,
Arndale/ iStock.com; illustration on p. 145 iStock.com/A-Digit

Distributed in Australia by:
MediaCom Education Inc, PO Box 610, Unley, SA 5061
Tel: 1 800 811 311 | admin@mediacom.org.au

Distributed in New Zealand by:
Scripture Union Wholesale, PO Box 760, Wellington 6140
Tel: 04 385 0421 | suwholesale@clear.net.nz

Acknowledgements

Scripture quotations marked with the following abbreviations are taken from the
version shown. NRSV: The New Revised Standard Version of the Bible, Anglicised
Edition, copyright © 1989, 1995 by the Division of Christian Education of the
National Council of the Churches of Christ in the USA. Used by permission. All
rights reserved. NIV: The Holy Bible, New International Version, Anglicised edition,
copyright © 1979, 1984, 2011 by Biblica. Used by permission of Hodder & Stoughton
Publishers, an Hachette UK company. All rights reserved. 'NIV' is a registered
trademark of Biblica. UK trademark number 1448790. KJV: The Authorised Version
of the Bible (The King James Bible), the rights in which are vested in the Crown, are
reproduced by permission of the Crown's Patentee, Cambridge University Press.
MSG: *The Message*, copyright © 1993, 1994, 1995, 1996, 2000, 2001, 2002 by Eugene
H. Peterson. Used by permission of NavPress. All rights reserved. Represented by
Tyndale House Publishers, Inc. NKJV: The New King James Version®. Copyright
© 1982 by Thomas Nelson. Used by permission. All rights reserved.

A catalogue record for this book is available from the British Library

Printed by Gutenberg Press, Tarxien, Malta

Suggestions for using *New Daylight*

Find a regular time and place, if possible, where you can read and pray undisturbed. Before you begin, take time to be still and perhaps use the BRF Prayer on page 6. Then read the Bible passage slowly (try reading it aloud if you find it over-familiar), followed by the comment. You can also use *New Daylight* for group study and discussion, if you prefer.

The prayer or point for reflection can be a starting point for your own meditation and prayer. Many people like to keep a journal to record their thoughts about a Bible passage and items for prayer. In *New Daylight* we also note the Sundays and some special festivals from the church calendar, to keep in step with the Christian year.

New Daylight and the Bible

New Daylight contributors use a range of Bible versions, and you will find a list of the versions used opposite. You are welcome to use your own preferred version alongside the passage printed in the notes. This can be particularly helpful if the Bible text has been abridged.

New Daylight affirms that the whole of the Bible is God's revelation to us, and we should read, reflect on and learn from every part of both Old and New Testaments. Usually the printed comment presents a straightforward 'thought for the day', but sometimes it may also raise questions rather than simply providing answers, as we wrestle with some of the more difficult passages of scripture.

New Daylight is also available in a deluxe edition (larger format). Visit your local Christian bookshop or BRF's online shop **brfonline.org.uk**. To obtain an audio version for the blind or partially sighted, contact Torch Trust for the Blind, Torch House, Torch Way, Northampton Road, Market Harborough LE16 9HL; +44 (0)1858 438260; **info@torchtrust.org**.

Comment on *New Daylight*

To send feedback, please email **enquiries@brf.org.uk**, phone **+44 (0)1865 319700** or write to the address shown opposite.

Writers in this issue

Amy Boucher Pye is a writer and speaker who runs the *Woman Alive* book club. She's the author of several books, including *Seven Ways to Pray* (SPCK, 2021) and *Celebrating Christmas* (BRF, 2021). Find her at **amyboucherpye.com**.

Tony Horsfall is a freelance trainer and retreat leader based in Yorkshire. He is an elder in his local church and the author of several books for BRF, including *Mentoring Conversations*, *Servant Ministry*, *Working from a Place of Rest* and *Spiritual Growth in a Time of Change*.

Lakshmi Jeffreys is the rector of a parish just outside Northampton. She combines this with being a wife, mother, friend, dog-walker, school governor and various other roles, within and beyond the wider church.

Murdo Macdonald is a molecular biologist, with over 20 years' experience working in research labs, including almost a decade serving with the Leprosy Mission in Nepal. Since 2008 Murdo has been based near Edinburgh, where he leads the Society, Religion and Technology Project of the Church of Scotland.

Michael Mitton works freelance in the areas of spirituality and mission. He is also an honorary canon of Derby Cathedral and is the NSM priest in charge of St Paul's Derby. He is author of *Restoring the Woven Cord* (third edition, BRF, 2019).

Stephen Rand worked with Tearfund and Open Doors, travelling widely. Now retired, he is the part-time web editor for the All Party Parliamentary Group for International Freedom of Religion or Belief.

Harry Smart is an Anglican priest. He has been a mental health and general hospital chaplain for 20 years, currently working in Scunthorpe. He leads mindfulness retreats and sessions for NHS staff.

Sheila Walker has been a teacher, editor, single parent, author, information officer, grandmother... and is currently serving as associate minister with three rural churches.

Sally Welch writes…

As I write this, the smell of apples simmering with cloves and nutmeg drifts into my study; it is harvest time and the gardens, hedgerows and fields of the countryside are full, almost to overflowing, with produce. Our small town is making the best of this season and has established a fruit and vegetable exchange – people with over-productive fruit trees and vegetable patches can offload their surplus so that others who lack the space, time or expertise can enjoy garden-fresh food for free. In return, they offer flowers, eggs or simply their gratitude as they take home bags of plums or handfuls of tomatoes. Everyone benefits.

These biblical principles of hospitality and generosity are beautifully illustrated by Lakshmi Jeffreys as she explores eating together – one of the holy habits we are encouraged to develop as part of our Christian spirituality. She reminds us of the precious nature of the gift of food – one of many of God's gifts to us through his creation. Creation is also the theme of Michael Mitton's reflections, as he shares the importance of landscape in Celtic Christian spirituality, highlighting that 'death is never the end of the story' (p. 18). This message is sorely needed by Job, whose story of trial and suffering is redeemed through his own growth in understanding and God's grace. Tony Horsfall treads a sympathetic and sensitive path through the chapters of Job, reassuring us of God's good purposes even when we cannot understand them.

When the apples are cooked, I will add blackberries and freeze the result. In the cold darkness of winter, their taste will remind me of golden autumn harvests as well as the spring sowing and summer cultivation, which have gone before them. So too will Isaiah's words, as he reminds us of the care God has shown his people in the past, comforting us as we face the troubles and challenges that are a part of human living. As the prophet looked forward to the Messiah, so we rejoice in the fulfilment of that prophecy in the birth of Christ, so lovingly shown to us in the gospels, as Amy Boucher Pye and Sheila Walker demonstrate in their reflections, which take us through Advent into the joy and hope of Christmas.

My prayers for you are for a joyful harvest of reflection, understanding and love as you journey through these notes this season.

Sally Ann Welch

The BRF Prayer

Almighty God,
you have taught us that your word is a lamp for our feet
and a light for our path. Help us, and all who prayerfully
read your word, to deepen our fellowship with you
and with each other through your love.
And in so doing may we come to know you more fully,
love you more truly, and follow more faithfully
in the steps of your Son Jesus Christ, who lives and reigns
with you and the Holy Spirit, one God forevermore.
Amen

Were you there? BRF celebrates its centenary in 2022 and we'd love you to share your BRF memories with us. We've already heard from supporters with wonderful stories. Beryl Fudge attended our 25th anniversary service in Westminster Central Hall in 1947, in the presence of the Queen Mother and Princess Margaret. Catharine Heron was prepared for confirmation in 1945 by our founder, Canon Leslie Mannering, and still has his duplicated notes in their original brown cardboard folder.

Do you have a BRF story to tell, whether of events, people, books or Bible reading notes? Please email **eley.mcainsh@brf.org.uk**, call **01865 319708** or write to **Eley McAinsh** at BRF, 15 The Chambers, Vineyard, Abingdon, OX14 3FE, United Kingdom.

All creation is groaning:
Celtic Christian spirituality

One of the features of Celtic Christian spirituality that is frequently admired is its connectedness to creation. The culture into which the likes of Brigid, Ninian, David and Hilda (early Celtic saints) preached the gospel was one where the rhythms of the seasons were all important and lives depended on the success of the harvest. Like many indigenous cultures, there was a great respect for the land and an awareness of a spiritual dimension to creation.

Many pre-Christian Celts were pantheists – their gods were enshrined in creation. As the Christian evangelists shared the gospel in these communities, they celebrated this instinctive respect for creation and openness to the spiritual vitality of the earth. They drew the people away from worshipping the things *of* creation into a deep love *for* the creator of all things. But in doing so, they saw no reason to discard the inherent respect for nature. In other parts of Christendom, there was a growing suspicion of the natural world, as there was of human nature. Creation was indeed celebrated as beautiful and could reflect the glory of God, but it had been badly damaged at the fall and therefore could not be trusted. As time went on, creation was seen as being primarily there to serve the needs of humans who sought to dominate it.

Sadly, this is the view that generally prevailed over the Celtic respect for creation. With the Industrial Revolution, the abuse of our planet reached a new level. Only relatively recently has the world woken up to the consequences of treating our planet so badly, and there is a growing concern that climate change is becoming a severe threat to the planet and the humans who dwell here.

Celtic Christian spirituality not only holds a deep respect for creation, it also integrates the natural world with spiritual life. Though they were not without their faults, we have much to learn from our Celtic forbears, and in the coming days, we shall be considering how they might be our tutors in the tasks of loving this glorious yet vulnerable world in which God has placed us and discerning his works within it.

MICHAEL MITTON

7

The Spirit

For the creation waits with eager longing for the revealing of the children of God; for the creation was subjected to futility, not of its own will but by the will of the one who subjected it, in hope that the creation itself will be set free from its bondage to decay and will obtain the freedom of the glory of the children of God. We know that the whole creation has been groaning in labour pains until now; and not only the creation, but we ourselves, who have the first fruits of the Spirit, groan inwardly while we wait for adoption, the redemption of our bodies.

This passage may be the clearest biblical example of the interaction between humans, creation and the Spirit. All three – creation (v. 22), humans (v. 23) and the Spirit (v. 26) – find themselves groaning. We are joined in this longing.

The apostle Paul tells us that creation is longing for the revealing of the children of God (v. 19). Think back for a moment to the glorious story of creation, which is followed by the disastrous rebellion of Adam and Eve. God says to Adam, 'Cursed is the ground because of you' (Genesis 3:17). These terrible words tell us that there is a direct correlation between the spiritual health of humans and the well-being of our planet. If we choose to turn against the ways of God, it is not just we who suffer, but our planet also. The vast amounts of plastic washing into our oceans and the wanton destruction of rainforests are two clear examples of this. The earth is cursed by our lifestyles.

But there is good news. If we follow the Spirit, we are children of God (Romans 8:14), and it is these children that creation is longing to see. Why? Because Spirit-led followers of Christ develop a new sensitivity to creation. The work of the cross and resurrection has reversed the curse of the fall. Now humans will no longer be a curse to the earth, but a blessing to it.

Christians, of all people, should be alive to the groans of creation. You, who carry the Spirit, are a sign of hope.

How might the Spirit direct you to be a blessing to the earth today?

MICHAEL MITTON

Mountain

Six days later, Jesus took with him Peter and James and his brother John and led them up a high mountain, by themselves. And he was transfigured before them, and his face shone like the sun, and his clothes became dazzling white. Suddenly there appeared to them Moses and Elijah, talking with him. Then Peter said to Jesus, 'Lord, it is good for us to be here; if you wish, I will make three dwellings here, one for you, one for Moses, and one for Elijah.' While he was still speaking, suddenly a bright cloud overshadowed them, and from the cloud a voice said, 'This is my Son, the Beloved; with him I am well pleased; listen to him!'

Over the next few days, we shall look at some well-known features of creation. Today, we think about the mountain. Matthew has a particular interest in mountains, and today's reading is perhaps the best-known of his mountain stories.

Anyone who loves climbing hills or mountains hopes for a clear day so they can enjoy the views. A hilltop affords a different perspective and gives you the chance to see into the far distance. Jesus often taught on a mountain, and there people began to see life from a different perspective. On the Mount of Transfiguration, the disciples' eyes were not drawn to the view of the land below them, but to the man standing before them. They saw him in a completely different light. Mountains are often places of revelation.

Not far from St Austell in Cornwall is Roche Rock. This is a striking rocky outcrop that rises up over 60 feet, and you can climb up to the remains of a medieval chapel dedicated to St Michael. The chapel was likely built over the site of an earlier Celtic chapel, for such a site was favoured by mystics and hermits who longed to gain fresh perspectives on God and his creation. These were the 'see-ers' who gave time in watchful prayer to see the things beyond our normal eyesight.

There is much in God's creation that draws us into seeing the things of God. High places can broaden our vision.

How might you see the things of God in his creation today?

MICHAEL MITTON

Desert

Jesus, full of the Holy Spirit, returned from the Jordan and was led by the Spirit in the wilderness, where for forty days he was tempted by the devil. He ate nothing at all during those days, and when they were over, he was famished… Then Jesus, filled with the power of the Spirit, returned to Galilee, and a report about him spread through all the surrounding country.

The Celtic church was influenced by the powerful renewal movement that took place in the deserts of Egypt in the fourth century onwards. They were intrigued by the concept of the desert, and many of them sought their own *dysart* place. They modelled this on the story of Jesus' days of fasting in the wilderness.

In Ireland and the UK, there are no barren, hot wastelands such as there are in Egypt. However, the Celtic church looked for equivalent testing places. If you were to visit the Ring of Kerry in the south of Ireland, you might take a boat out to the island of Skellig Michael. There you can climb the 600 steps to the little monastic village that was founded possibly as early as the sixth century. St Cuthbert also sought out his *dysart* on Farne Island. Such places were seen to be powerhouses – places of intercessory prayer and fasting and battling with evil.

Those who sought out these *dysart* places were not doing it for selfish reasons. They believed they were following the example of Jesus. They were tackling spiritual foes head on, and they were also expectant of being refuelled by the Holy Spirit so that they, and those for whom they prayed, would be empowered for the preaching of the gospel.

Deserts are places where we are deprived of our normal comforts. In such vulnerability, we have to face our weaknesses. Stripped of inessentials, we recognise our need of God. Further, the desert can be the place of new encounters with the Spirit and becoming empowered for mission.

Some deserts are forced on us by circumstances. Sometimes we choose to journey into the desert. Either way, the desert is full of possibilities.

What does the desert mean to you? How might a desert become a place of encounter with God's Spirit?

MICHAEL MITTON

Garden

Look to Abraham your father and to Sarah who bore you; for he was but one when I called him, but I blessed him and made him many. For the Lord will comfort Zion; he will comfort all her waste places, and will make her wilderness like Eden, her desert like the garden of the Lord; joy and gladness will be found in her, thanksgiving and the voice of song.

These words from Isaiah were first preached to the exiles in Babylon who had trudged across a desert to their captivity. But here the prophet brings a message of hope, that God will convert the desert into the garden of the Lord. Eden was the blessed garden, the place for which all humans have been homesick since Adam and Eve were exiled. The garden of the Lord is the world as it was always meant to be.

Many of us love being in our gardens, enjoying the thrilling fertility of life just beyond our backdoors. There is an instinctive love for the beauty of creation in the human heart. It is also a longing to see the earth flourishing and being at its best.

Kevin was a mystic poet who lived in the sixth century and founded a monastery in a most beautiful place in Ireland now called Glendalough. A visitor to this site today can see the site of 'Kevin's desert', the place by the lake to which he liked to retreat. To get there you travel down the Green Road that runs along the edge of the forest. Many feel a sense of peace and blessing at Glendalough. It feels like it carries resonances of the garden of the Lord.

There is space in the kingdom of God for both gardens and deserts. The gardens remind us of how things are supposed to be. They can evoke yearning in us. The more we love gardens, the more we grieve when land that should be garden becomes wasteland. A true vision for the garden of the Lord will mean we cannot bear to see creation harmed. Such sorrow may open us to a call to be part of the healing of the land.

How does this theme of the garden of the Lord touch you today?

MICHAEL MITTON

Wells

So Isaac departed from there and camped in the valley of Gerar and settled there. Isaac dug again the wells of water that had been dug in the days of his father Abraham; for the Philistines had stopped them up after the death of Abraham; and he gave them the names that his father had given them… He moved from there and dug another well, and they did not quarrel over it; so he called it Rehoboth, saying, 'Now the Lord has made room for us, and we shall be fruitful in the land.'

Isaac finds himself in the land of the Philistines, where his father once lived. He discovered that all the wells Abraham had dug had been filled in, so he unearthed them and began to dig new ones all the way to Beersheba. For people without the luxury of running tap water, wells are essential. But this story is not just about physical water. There is an allusion to the spiritual waters of life here. Isaac is tapping into the waters of life discovered by his father. In John 4, Jesus also picks up this connection of wells and living water.

The Celtic church loved wells, and many can still be found today. They recognised the powerful image of life gushing up from the deep waters of the earth. The stories of those early pioneers of faith can act like wells for us today. We can unearth those stories and be inspired and enlivened by them. We can take a trip to such places as St Non's well, near St David's in Pembrokeshire, and be inspired by the story of her and the son she birthed near this well, David of Wales.

But wells also make us aware of how water is a scarce commodity for too many people on this planet. Wells are great places to intercede for those who have to travel long distances to collect fresh water. They are also places of listening, where we may hear how God might be calling us to be part of the answer to this need.

Think of a well or a stream you have visited. What might the Spirit of God want to unearth in your life? Intercede for those who lack fresh water.

MICHAEL MITTON

Sea

After we had sailed across the sea that is off Cilicia and Pamphylia, we came to Myra in Lycia. There the centurion found an Alexandrian ship bound for Italy and put us on board. We sailed slowly for a number of days and arrived with difficulty off Cnidus, and as the wind was against us, we sailed under the lee of Crete off Salmone. Sailing past it with difficulty, we came to a place called Fair Havens, near the city of Lasea.

There are many sea stories in the Bible, and they are often associated with threat and adventure. For example, Moses and the Red Sea; Jonah and the whale; Jesus and the stormy Sea of Galilee; and, here, Paul on the Mediterranean Sea. In these stories, the sea is often perilous, and yet it is also a place of journeying, risk-taking, the forging of new faith, with discoveries of the protection of God. Acts 27 is a thrilling chapter, where Paul's faith triumphs over the fear of the sailors. These opening verses of Acts 27 give hints that the coming sea journey is going to be rough. By the end of the chapter, after many nautical terrors, the ship is wrecked off Malta, but everyone is safe.

The greatest sea story from the Celtic era is that of the sixth-century Brendan of Clonfert, who, with his companions, embarked on a transatlantic adventure in a small boat. The accounts of this journey were no doubt embellished, but what shines out from the story is Brendan's faith and longing for an adventure with God. He is rewarded with seeing things he never imagined seeing and with discoveries about the world, himself and God. It is worth checking out his wonderful prayer, which ends with:

Shall I take my tiny coracle across the wide sparkling ocean?
O King of the glorious heaven, shall I go of my own choice upon the sea?
O Christ, help me with the wild waves!

Brendan chose his adventure. Paul's was chosen for him. Both, however, knew the presence and protection of God.

Read the whole story of Paul's sea journey in Acts 27. What might God be saying to you through it? Are you being called to new adventures?

MICHAEL MITTON

Consecration

Then the Lord said to Cain, 'Where is your brother Abel?' He said, 'I do not know; am I my brother's keeper?' And the Lord said, 'What have you done? Listen; your brother's blood is crying out to me from the ground! And now you are cursed from the ground, which has opened its mouth to receive your brother's blood from your hand. When you till the ground, it will no longer yield to you its strength; you will be a fugitive and a wanderer on the earth.'

After the calamitous story of the fall in Genesis 3, we come to the grim story of sibling jealousy between Cain and Abel, which results in the first account of murder in the Bible. It is all the more appalling because the story of the perfect Eden is still ringing in our ears. That story was one of a totally blessed land. This story tells of a cursed land, tainted with human blood.

Among the many insights this story gives us is the fact that land is affected by human activity. Even in our 21st-century sophisticated world, many people still testify to some places feeling particularly peaceful, while others feel disturbed or haunted.

The seventh-century Cedd was asked to found a monastery. We are told by the historian Bede that he looked for land despoiled by 'earlier crimes'. The purpose of this was to transform the spiritual state of the land through a process of consecration, which he did through prayer and fasting. Quite how he discerned these earlier crimes we do not know. Maybe such crimes were well known, or maybe it was through his prayer and listening. Either way, he saw it as his job to change the place from being cursed to being blessed.

These early missionaries believed that the Christian church had a responsibility to bless the land and to heal it where they discovered it to be in some way cursed or damaged by human sinfulness. As we look across our planet, we see so many places wounded by humans. Creation is longing for the children of God to take up their responsibility to pray and act for the healing of the land.

How might you be a blessing to the land today?

MICHAEL MITTON

Animals

When the donkey saw the angel of the Lord, it lay down under Balaam; and Balaam's anger was kindled, and he struck the donkey with his staff. Then the Lord opened the mouth of the donkey, and it said to Balaam, 'What have I done to you, that you have struck me these three times?' Balaam said to the donkey, 'Because you have made a fool of me! I wish I had a sword in my hand! I would kill you right now!' But the donkey said to Balaam, 'Am I not your donkey, which you have ridden all your life to this day? Have I been in the habit of treating you in this way?'

This story happens shortly before the entry into the promised land. Balak, the king of Moab, feels threatened by the large number of Israelites near his land and calls on Balaam, a diviner, to lay a curse on them. Balaam heads off on his donkey but is prevented from travelling further when his donkey stubbornly stops in the road. The road is blocked by an angel. Balaam, who is supposed to be a seer, fails to see the angel, while the donkey has no problem seeing the divine figure. We then have the conversation reported in today's passage. In the end, Balaam does see the angel, and all is well.

A story like this tells us there is a clear recognition that animals, created by God, are capable of spiritual sensitivity. In the early Celtic church, there are numerous stories of animals detecting the presence of God in his people, thereby losing both fear and aggression: for example, Kentigern and his robin; Kevin and the blackbird; Cuthbert and the otters; Columbanus with the wolves; and Melangell, in whose presence, it was said, all wild animals became peaceful. We can easily dismiss these as fairy tales, and there is surely some fabrication in some of the stories. But what is clear is that these early missionaries believed that the animal kingdom had a sensitivity to God, could live in harmony with Spirit-filled humans and could also be used by God to serve his purposes.

What is God saying to you today about his creatures?

MICHAEL MITTON

Angels

In Caesarea there was a man named Cornelius, a centurion of the Italian Cohort, as it was called. He was a devout man who feared God with all his household; he gave alms generously to the people and prayed constantly to God. One afternoon at about three o'clock he had a vision in which he clearly saw an angel of God coming in and saying to him, 'Cornelius.' He stared at him in terror and said, 'What is it, Lord?' He answered, 'Your prayers and your alms have ascended as a memorial before God.'

There are frequent references to angels in both the Old and New Testaments. Cornelius is not alone in his experience of feeling terrified at the sight of an angel. To see an angel in this way takes him straight into the world of the supernatural, and for most humans this is very unfamiliar territory. Nonetheless, Cornelius does not run for cover and is open to believing that such things as angels exist. He has an open mind and an open heart, and the result for him is salvation (see the rest of the chapter).

Any reading of the accounts of the early Celtic missionaries will soon lead you to a story involving an angel. Take the sixth-century Columba, for example, whose mother, when carrying him, met an angel in a dream who prophesied about her son. Columba became a great church-planter in Ireland, and he said he particularly loved Derry, not least because it was a place full of angels. He eventually made his way to Iona and founded a remarkable mission base there. Visitors to Iona today can see the Hill of Angels, the place where Columba purportedly used to meet the angels and worship God with them.

The Bible is clear that these messengers of heaven are quite at home on this earth. Many people have testified to seeing angels in this world. But even if we have not seen them with our eyes, we can acknowledge their presence by faith and be grateful in our hearts that such servants of God are here to assist us.

What are your thoughts about angels?
How might their presence help you today?

MICHAEL MITTON

Glory

In the year that King Uzziah died, I saw the Lord sitting on a throne, high and lofty; and the hem of his robe filled the temple. Seraphs were in attendance above him; each had six wings: with two they covered their faces, and with two they covered their feet, and with two they flew. And one called to another and said: 'Holy, holy, holy is the Lord of hosts; the whole earth is full of his glory.' The pivots on the thresholds shook at the voices of those who called, and the house filled with smoke.

Isaiah was to become one of the greatest visionary prophets ever, but presumably, at this stage of his life and career, such a vision as this must have shaken him to the core. To behold these magnificent angels would have been astounding. He would not have been surprised to hear these creatures of heaven worshipping God. But what may have surprised him was to hear them exulting in the fact that the glory of God could be found on this earth. Isaiah is witnessing the angels delighting in the fact that the sacred glows in the secular.

Celtic spirituality does acknowledge that there is darkness in this world and that much harm has been done through human sinfulness and the influence of evil. However, it also affirms that much in this world is blessed and can be radiant with the life of heaven.

Many people are familiar with the prayer attributed to Patrick, often known as St Patrick's Breastplate. It is a profoundly Christ-centred prayer, and yet in the middle we find these words, 'I arise today, through the strength of heaven, the light of the sun, the radiance of the moon, the splendour of fire, the speed of lightning, the swiftness of wind, the depth of the sea, the stability of the earth, the firmness of rock.' The collection of ancient prayers and blessings known as the *Carmina Gadelica* also recognise God-blessed creation as a strength and resource. To witness such glory in creation nearly always requires us to slow down and become attentive.

How can you become more open to seeing the glory of God in creation?

MICHAEL MITTON

Death and resurrection

When they heard these things, they became enraged and ground their teeth at Stephen. But filled with the Holy Spirit, he gazed into heaven and saw the glory of God and Jesus standing at the right hand of God. 'Look,' he said, 'I see the heavens opened and the Son of Man standing at the right hand of God!' But they covered their ears, and with a loud shout all rushed together against him. Then they dragged him out of the city and began to stone him.

For those who loved Stephen, his violent and untimely death would have been shocking and agonising. However, the manner of his passing would have given them much comfort, for during his final moments, his eyes were opened to see a wonderful vision of Christ and heaven.

The stories we have of the deaths of the early Celtic missionaries resound with a similar sense of the message and power of resurrection invading the experience of human death. The seventh-century Hilda of Whitby died after being afflicted with a debilitating sickness for six years. In a monastery 13 miles away, a nun was awoken from sleep by the sound of a bell. She saw a light pouring down from heaven, and in the midst of this radiant light, she saw Hilda being escorted to heaven by angels. The night Aidan died, the young Cuthbert was on a hillside nearby and saw the spirit of Aidan being taken to heaven by angels. These early Christians saw a great deal of death, not least due to plagues. But their confidence in resurrection life is steadfast.

Such stories affirm the message we see so clearly in creation – that death is never the end of the story. Spring resurrection always follows winter death, and one day the whole of creation will experience its own resurrection in the new heaven and earth (Revelation 21:1). The loved ones of Stephen, Hilda and Aidan grieved deeply. But they were also given glimpses of the glory to come. This world is our home, and as such it is to be treasured and loved. But it always has to be held in the context of the world to come.

How does the vision of the future affect your care for this world?

MICHAEL MITTON

Isaiah 1—45: prophet of hope

I must confess to having held in the past a very shallow vision of what a prophet is. For me, a prophet was a man with a straggling beard and untidy hair, wearing a long, eccentric garment and wandering about a Mediterranean marketplace ignored by almost everyone. I suspect this view came from having watched *Monty Python's Life of Brian* at too young an age! Fortunately, further study has enabled me to review that vision and to realise the vital importance that prophets hold not just in biblical times, but for Christians today.

Prophets can come in all shapes and sizes. What they say might be offensive to some, but the true prophet must be honest to their message. Prophets stand outside the current situation in order to comment on it; they try to retain objectivity in order to preach wisdom. The role of a prophet is demanding, rigorous and vital, as they hold up a mirror to society, enabling us to see ourselves clearly, challenging our often narrow view of what is going on.

Isaiah the prophet preached in Judea (the southern kingdom) circa 740–701BC. He witnessed at first hand the corruption of the ruling class, which led to the poor getting poorer. He warned against the threat of invaders and conquerors, and his prophecies came true when, in 722, the Assyrians overran the northern part of the kingdom. Yet despite the bleakness of the political and social climate, Isaiah's words are filled with hope. Perhaps this is ultimately the true job of a prophet – to remind us when times are good that efforts must be made to maintain standards of justice and integrity, and to support us when our situation becomes challenging, encouraging us with memories of past happiness and helping us to look forward to a better future.

Isaiah is a huge book and filled with material for the reflective writer. In order to restrict my choice, I have used those readings that are part of the Anglican lectionary. They are particularly hopeful passages, as many of them are set for the seasons of Lent and Advent – those times when we pause to reflect on our journey to this time and also look forward in hope to the fulfilment of all God's promises in Christ.

SALLY WELCH

Washing day

Wash yourselves; make yourselves clean; remove the evil of your doings from before my eyes; cease to do evil, learn to do good; seek justice, rescue the oppressed, defend the orphan, plead for the widow. Come now, let us argue it out, says the Lord: though your sins are like scarlet, they shall be like snow; though they are red like crimson, they shall become like wool.

I have spent quite a lot of my life doing laundry – a husband and four children have seen to that! It has not, however, been an unrewarding task. There is the satisfaction of seeing dirty clothes emerging clean and fresh from the washing machine, the lovely smell of line-dried laundry and the quiet pleasure of folding small garments to put away ready for another day. So, too, the process of examining our own lives prior to 'washing ourselves' can have its own joys – looking carefully at our habits and patterns of living, discerning what we should change and which areas need to be made clean.

I am also aware of the effect of washing just one red sock with white garments – everything comes out pink, the stain of one object affecting the whole load. Similarly, just one area of our lives in which we are living less than righteously can impact so much else. So we need to be rigorous in our examination.

Once 'sorted', we can bring our sorrows and our failures, our guilts and our omissions, like so much dirty laundry, before the Lord, confessing to those acts that stain our lives and asking for his forgiveness and cleansing. And he has promised us that he will do this. By his death, Christ paid the price of this act of washing. Through his gift of baptism, Jesus gives us the grace to come before him time after time and ask his forgiveness. Then what our joy will be like, when our tattered and stained garments are made whole and clean again, the scarlet of our sins washed white as wool.

What can wash away my sin?
Nothing but the blood of Jesus.
What can make me whole again?
Nothing but the blood of Jesus.
(Robert Lowry, 1826–99)

SALLY WELCH

A vision of peace

The word that Isaiah son of Amoz saw concerning Judah and Jerusalem. In days to come the mountain of the Lord's house shall be established as the highest of the mountains, and shall be raised above the hills; all the nations shall stream to it. Many peoples shall come and say, 'Come, let us go up to the mountain of the Lord, to the house of the God of Jacob; that he may teach us his ways and that we may walk in his paths.' For out of Zion shall go forth instruction, and the word of the Lord from Jerusalem. He shall judge between the nations, and shall arbitrate for many peoples; they shall beat their swords into ploughshares, and their spears into pruning-hooks; nation shall not lift up sword against nation, neither shall they learn war any more. O house of Jacob, come, let us walk in the light of the Lord!

How Isaiah's heart must have wept for the children of Israel. Threatened by Assyrians to the north and east and menaced by the Egyptians to the south and west, an atmosphere of fear and uncertainty pervaded the land. Living in turbulent times, the rulers of the house of Israel were preoccupied with getting and keeping, with defending their territory and accumulating wealth. This attitude percolated down to the people – no longer were widows and orphans being cared for, as every person was preoccupied with providing enough for themselves and their families, never mind those who had no one to protect them from the effects of poverty or ill health.

What to say to this anxious, threatened people, cowering behind the flimsy walls of material possessions, hoping that misfortune will not spot them and take what little they have? It does no good to breathe more threats to those already under fire. What people need in times like this is hope.

And so a beautiful vision is born – of people turning their faces away from the darkness of despair and selfishness and focusing instead on the 'highest of the mountains' (v. 2), raising their hopes beyond the everyday toil of survival and breathing in the pure air of hope.

Lord, help me to keep the vision of peace alive in my heart
and in the hopes of others.

SALLY WELCH

Soul-gardening

Let me sing for my beloved my love-song concerning his vineyard: My beloved had a vineyard on a very fertile hill. He dug it and cleared it of stones, and planted it with choice vines; he built a watch-tower in the midst of it, and hewed out a wine vat in it; he expected it to yield grapes, but it yielded wild grapes. And now, inhabitants of Jerusalem and people of Judah, judge between me and my vineyard. What more was there to do for my vineyard that I have not done in it? When I expected it to yield grapes, why did it yield wild grapes?

One of the delights of living in a vicarage is the generosity of the garden one can be allocated. Even in the middle of a city, I have rejoiced in a larger-than-average plot of land for such an urban environment. I am not so fond of growing flowers, but I love to grow vegetables – carefully planting the seeds, tenderly picking out the strongest seedlings and potting them on, planting them out in a double-dug vegetable patch and subjecting myself to the discipline of watering and weeding. The final result – of freshly picked vegetables – is to my mind more full of taste than even the best produce of a farmer's market, seasoned as it is with the satisfaction of a job well done.

My sympathy is fully engaged, therefore, with this metaphor of a vine-yard, carefully nurtured and tended, planted with choice vines after the back-breaking effort of digging and clearing. What anticipation must have been felt for the expected crop, only for it all to go sour – literally in this case, as only tiny, bitter grapes are produced.

Are there areas in our own lives that have yielded only withered crops? Are there relationships that have been tended and nurtured but have produced only unhappiness and hurt? Sometimes there is more work that can be done – soil can be refreshed and good fruits appear. At other times, we must allow ourselves to leave the unproductive and move on.

---

*'God, grant me the serenity to accept the things I cannot change,
courage to change the things I can and wisdom to know the difference'
(Reinhold Niebuhr, 1892–1971).*

SALLY WELCH

Is it I?

And I said: 'Woe is me! I am lost, for I am a man of unclean lips, and I live among a people of unclean lips; yet my eyes have seen the King, the Lord of hosts!' Then one of the seraphs flew to me, holding a live coal that had been taken from the altar with a pair of tongs. The seraph touched my mouth with it and said: 'Now that this has touched your lips, your guilt has departed and your sin is blotted out.' Then I heard the voice of the Lord saying, 'Whom shall I send, and who will go for us?' And I said, 'Here am I; send me!'

The chorus of the well-known hymn 'I the Lord of sea and sky' uses the words from this passage and 1 Samuel 3:4 ('Then the Lord called, "Samuel! Samuel!" and he said, "Here I am!"'). Written by Dan Schutte in 1981 when he was at theological college, the hymn was voted the UK's tenth favourite in 2019.

When I was at theological college, I felt that we sang it all the time – and I hated it! Every time the chorus rolled round, I would be frantically thinking, 'I don't think it's me that God is calling. How can it be? I am so bad at so much – what sort of priest will I make and how can God possibly use me?' The phrase 'imposter syndrome' might have been invented for me.

Over the years, the raw pain of this feeling has dulled somewhat. I have learnt to take heart from the things I can do and not to weep too much over the things I can't. I hope I have encouraged others to do the same. And at the heart of my ministry has always been the same call, 'Whom shall I send?', and the same response, 'Send me.'

Send me, with my inadequacies and my failures, my gifts and my strengths. Send me, and I will do my best to share your love with those around me. Send me, and I will learn to trust in your strength and the way you work with the most unpromising material to accomplish your vision.

'Samuel said, "Speak, for your servant is listening"' (1 Samuel 3:10).

SALLY WELCH

Walking in darkness

But there will be no gloom for those who were in anguish. In the former time he brought into contempt the land of Zebulun and the land of Naphtali, but in the latter time he will make glorious the way of the sea, the land beyond the Jordan, Galilee of the nations. The people who walked in darkness have seen a great light; those who lived in a land of deep darkness – on them light has shined.

What a powerful way of describing a situation involving long-term suffering! 'Walking in darkness' – how that resonates as we consider those times in our lives that involved chronic pain or sickness, mental fragility, relationship difficulties or death itself. A long journey, perhaps along a route not walked before, perhaps of necessity walked alone and always in the darkness of grief and pain. Into this darkness shines the light of the promise, the light that will 'make glorious' the route before us, casting aside the shadows and the sadness, and flooding the future with light and hope.

For Christians, this passage contains more than a mere hope – it contains a prophecy. Better than that, it contains a prophecy that is fulfilled in the birth, death and resurrection of Christ. The phrase 'Galilee of the nations' sounds like a bell, reverberating through the silence of our unhappiness, reminding us that on us the 'light' has already shined. 'The light shines in the darkness, and the darkness did not overcome it,' writes John at the beginning of his gospel (1:5), thus bringing into reality this heart-mending promise.

We need no longer walk alone in darkness, because Christ will always be our companion on the journey, however traumatic or grief-stricken it is. We need no longer worry about the route, because he has marked the way, branded it with love, showing us how to move forward in hope and expectancy. As we take our first steps in a renewed walk of hope and faith, let us ask God not only to guide us, but also, conscious of our weakness, to give us the grace to follow that guidance wherever it leads.

Heavenly Father, let me be a true child of your promise,
as I walk in the light of your love.

SALLY WELCH

Looking forward in hope

A shoot shall come out from the stump of Jesse, and a branch shall grow out of his roots. The spirit of the Lord shall rest on him, the spirit of wisdom and understanding... The wolf shall live with the lamb... the calf and the lion and the fatling together, and a little child shall lead them... They will not hurt or destroy on all my holy mountain; for the earth will be full of the knowledge of the Lord as the waters cover the sea.

In the Anglican lectionary, these verses are read on the second Sunday in Advent, a season of reflection and preparation. Towns and cities are filled with Christmas decorations and shoppers looking for that perfect gift for someone they love. Carols are being sung, interweaved with readings such as these, which look forward to a time of peace and mutual understanding. The atmosphere is one of rejoicing, hopefulness and celebration, and these verses reflect all this.

How extraordinary, therefore, that this was written during one of the most troubled times in the history of Israel! Between about 740 and 700BC, the Assyrian army overran the hill country of Israel, wreaking havoc wherever it went. People spent their lives in fear of the next atrocity. Planting crops was a waste of time, as who knew whether they would be harvested and by whom. Looking to the future was pointless, as all that could be seen was further destruction and horror.

Into the midst of all this, Isaiah breathes calm and hope. 'A better time is coming,' he tells his people. 'Right now you are exhausted and beaten. You cannot see any kind of future, let alone a good one.' But this is one of the tasks of a prophet – to keep his people looking forward, to encourage belief in a better, richer, more peaceful future, to promote positive thinking rather than despair. As members of the Christian community, it is one of our tasks too.

Heavenly Father, help me to keep believing in a better world, even when all the evidence seems against this. Help me to work actively to bring in a future I can be proud of.

SALLY WELCH

Singing for joy

You will say on that day: I will give thanks to you, O Lord, for though you were angry with me, your anger turned away, and you comforted me. Surely God is my salvation; I will trust, and will not be afraid, for the Lord God is my strength and my might; he has become my salvation. With joy you will draw water from the wells of salvation. And you will say on that day: Give thanks to the Lord, call on his name; make known his deeds among the nations; proclaim that his name is exalted. Sing praises to the Lord, for he has done gloriously; let this be known in all the earth. Shout aloud and sing for joy, O royal Zion, for great in your midst is the Holy One of Israel.

The first eleven chapters of Isaiah contain some of the most beautiful and comforting words that the Bible can produce. Amid the hardship and terrors that God's children are suffering, Isaiah holds out the promise of a restored Israel, offering us a vision of a return to Jerusalem, the holy city that will itself be transformed.

Of course, in the chapters to come, we will hear the prophet's criticisms of errant behaviour and turning away from the good paths, but chapter 12, here in its entirety, offers a pause into which we can pour our response of joy and thanksgiving at the love and care our creator has shown to us.

Particularly poignant are those first few words, 'You will say in that day' – encouraging words to start us off. Hesitant and anxious, unsure of how to begin, we are offered the first few phrases to set us on the right track. We can acknowledge our faults and God's subsequent anger, but we can also trust in his forgiveness. With that trust will come rejoicing and praise as we draw on those everlasting wells of salvation.

Praise to the Lord,
the Almighty, the king of creation.
O my soul, praise him,
for he is thy health and salvation.
All ye who hear, now to his temple draw near.
Join me in glad adoration.
(Joachim Neandor, 1650–80)

SALLY WELCH

Prophet of doom

Thus says the Lord God of hosts: Come, go to this steward, to Shebna, who is master of the household, and say to him: What right do you have here? Who are your relatives here, that you have cut out a tomb here for yourself, cutting a tomb on the height, and carving a habitation for yourself in the rock? The Lord is about to hurl you away violently, my man. He will seize firm hold of you, whirl you round and round, and throw you like a ball into a wide land; there you shall die, and there your splendid chariots shall lie, O you disgrace to your master's house!

For most of my selection from Isaiah, I have focused on the glorious promises of the prophet. Speaking encouragement during impossible times to hearten those who are despairing, the poetry of the author's vision and the promises of God's salvation have offered hope and trust in the future not just to those first listeners, but also to believers through the centuries.

He would be a lop-sided prophet, however, who only focused on the uplifting and cheerful while ignoring the errors and sins of his people. Indeed, he would be failing in his task to guide and lead if he were to leave unmentioned the ways in which God's people were going astray and not bothering to correct them.

In this passage, Shebna, the state secretary to King Hezekiah, during whose reign Isaiah prophesied, has committed serious errors in the eyes of Isaiah. The prophet reminds not only Shebna but also those of us reading today that we must be aware constantly of God's judgement against us when we act in ways that are not true or righteous. When we fail to respond to God's love by loving in our turn; when we do not offer charity to our neighbour or forgiveness to our families; when we act selfishly or are filled with hate, then we must expect God's anger to rebound upon us.

Fortunately, through Christ, we have also the promise of God's forgiveness that follows our repentance like rain after drought, refreshing and bringing new life and hope.

Crucified Christ, keep us from doing wrong; but when we do,
help us to seek forgiveness.

SALLY WELCH

Feasting on memories

On this mountain the Lord of hosts will make for all peoples a feast of rich food, a feast of well-matured wines, of rich food filled with marrow, of well-matured wines strained clear. And he will destroy on this mountain the shroud that is cast over all peoples, the sheet that is spread over all nations; he will swallow up death forever. Then the Lord God will wipe away the tears from all faces, and the disgrace of his people he will take away from all the earth, for the Lord has spoken.

It is well known that many of the celebrations recorded in the Bible involve food in some way. Religious festivals, battle triumphs, family reunions – all centre around feasting. The traditional way of showing hospitality and welcome was to share whatever food was available in the household, even when resources were scarce.

But this feast is different. Isaiah isn't remembering happier times, and he certainly isn't reporting current events. Once again the children of Israel are experiencing appalling suffering as wave after wave of Assyrian invaders swoop down on their land, laying waste to the countryside, destroying everything they had worked for. So what better time is there, in fact, to look forward to the redemption of a promise, the enactment of a covenant. Just when it seems that God has forgotten his children, then it is that his children should hold fast to the belief that God will never abandon them. No matter what has gone wrong in the past, no matter how many times his people have strayed from the path, the promise of better times still holds good.

It is good to revisit the past – there is much we can learn from past sins and errors. It is good to inhabit the present, as it is in the 'now' that we will experience God's loving care most fully. But it is also good to hold on to a vision of the future, to look forward to a time when all our tears will be wiped away from our face by God himself, as he seats us at his banqueting table and invites us to rejoice with him.

God of the past and the present, keep me believing in the future.

SALLY WELCH

Making firm

The wilderness and the dry land shall be glad, the desert shall rejoice and blossom; like the crocus it shall blossom abundantly, and rejoice with joy and singing. The glory of Lebanon shall be given to it, the majesty of Carmel and Sharon. They shall see the glory of the Lord, the majesty of our God. Strengthen the weak hands, and make firm the feeble knees. Say to those who are of a fearful heart, 'Be strong, do not fear! Here is your God.'

This passage always reminds me of a former parishioner of mine who had a knee operation. She made it her declared goal to be walking normally in the time expected by her surgeon. She exercised diligently, did all those boring physio exercises that are so tedious but so necessary and continued with her daily routine – joking with me at morning prayer about asking God to 'make firm the feeble knees'. Needless to say, she recovered well within the predicted time, and indeed astonished her surgeon with the speed of her recovery. She became an example to others, encouraging those undergoing similar operations, supporting them in their anxiety and pain.

The prophet Isaiah holds out more promises to us here – more hope for the hopeless, those trapped in situations of conflict or pain, suffering or despair. But perhaps another injunction as well – 'Be strong, do not fear!' Perhaps this is a reminder that God is always prepared to keep his part of the covenant – to love, care for and defend his children – but also that there is a counterpart to that. A covenant requires two parties to keep it; it must be honoured by both sides or it will fall apart.

My lovely parishioner took on board the instructions of her surgeon and kept to the agreement to exercise diligently in order for the knee to heal properly. She then held out this hope of healing to others, pointing to her own recovery in order to help them in theirs. What could be achieved in our relationships and communities if we strengthened our 'weak hands' and held them out to be used by God to lift up others?

God of covenants and courage, help me to keep to my part of the promise.

SALLY WELCH

Path-makers

Comfort, O comfort my people, says your God. Speak tenderly to Jerusalem, and cry to her that she has served her term, that her penalty is paid, that she has received from the Lord's hand double for all her sins. A voice cries out: 'In the wilderness prepare the way of the Lord, make straight in the desert a highway for our God. Every valley shall be lifted up, and every mountain and hill be made low; the uneven ground shall become level, and the rough places a plain. Then the glory of the Lord shall be revealed, and all people shall see it together, for the mouth of the Lord has spoken.'

I am writing this early in the morning in a little hut in the corner of a field. I am on holiday with part of my family, and creeping away before everyone else is awake gives me precious reflection time before the chaos of the day. The countryside that surrounds me is endless trees, rivers and hills: it's a marvellous place to walk – or would be if the youngest wasn't in a pushchair. We take it in turns to lift, carry, jolt the buggy up hills, through streams and over rough ground. Nobody minds the effort, however; we don't want anyone to be left out, and the price for this is happily paid.

Isaiah points a suffering people towards easier times – times when the struggle simply to survive will no longer be so desperate; when the spiritual, physical and emotional paths that God's children walk will be made level; when we will gather, rejoicing to celebrate our presence in his company. Until then, however, is it not our role to help others on the journey – to guide and comfort those for whom the route is difficult and full of suffering? Just as John the Baptist prepared the way for Christ, so we, through our words and actions, can be signposts to a new way of living and sharing.

Lord God, help me to be a herald of the good tidings you bring.
May I be a path-maker, a route-smoother, helping others to walk
the path until all ways are made level.

SALLY WELCH

Grasshopper vision

Have you not known? Have you not heard? Has it not been told you from the beginning? Have you not understood from the foundations of the earth? It is he who sits above the circle of the earth, and its inhabitants are like grasshoppers; who stretches out the heavens like a curtain, and spreads them like a tent to live in; who brings princes to naught, and makes the rulers of the earth as nothing… To whom then will you compare me, or who is my equal? says the Holy One. Lift up your eyes on high and see: Who created these? He who brings out their host and numbers them, calling them all by name; because he is great in strength, mighty in power, not one is missing.

One of my regular walks takes me through a meadow edged with a small woodland, which has been carefully set aside as part of a nature reserve. Every season brings something new – the call of nesting birds, the arrival of the first spring flowers, the crispness of fallen leaves and the silence of snow-covered trees. In the heat of the summer, it is my favourite place to go; every step stirs up clouds of butterflies and insects, and pausing even for a moment leads to one's clothing being covered with tiny grasshoppers.

It is fun to bend right down and see the world as these small creatures do – blades of grass towering above their heads, tiny pebbles like boulders, drops of dew like vast cataracts of water. Aren't we like grasshoppers to the creator of the world – so small, so insignificant? Beside the power of God, princes and rulers are as nothing, we are told. It is easy, perhaps, to feel subdued and ignored, worthless and useless. But no! Instead, we are reminded that our great God calls us by name; he knows each one of us individually and has a purpose for us that only we can fulfil.

Creator God, help me not to be a grasshopper, so overwhelmed by the little things of everyday life that I fail to rejoice in the big picture of your love for me.

SALLY WELCH

Take my life

Thus says God, the Lord, who created the heavens and stretched them out, who spread out the earth and what comes from it, who gives breath to the people upon it and spirit to those who walk in it: I am the Lord, I have called you in righteousness, I have taken you by the hand and kept you; I have given you as a covenant to the people, a light to the nations, to open the eyes that are blind, to bring out the prisoners from the dungeon, from the prison those who sit in darkness. I am the Lord, that is my name; my glory I give to no other, nor my praise to idols. See, the former things have come to pass, and new things I now declare; before they spring forth, I tell you of them.

Writing these reflections has caused me to think a lot about my own calling – how it emerged and how I have walked in it. For that is what Isaiah is prompting us to do, isn't it? He's calling to each one of us, reminding us of the greatness of the God that we serve, of God's incredible love for each and every one of us and the precious nature of the covenant he has made with us, his people.

We have been cherished, protected, guided, encouraged. We have been reminded of our obligations to God and to each other. And we have also been reminded of the consequences when we forget our obligations and fail to value God's covenant. But most of all we have been called – to serve God in whatever way we can, to celebrate his glory and to work for his kingdom.

What inspiring words we read here! What a challenge we are given! What a responsibility! As we reflect on our own journey, we can look back to the 'former things' that have come to pass, and look forward to the 'new things', in which we can play a part, fulfilling our calling as 'a light to the nations'.

Take my life, and let it be
Consecrated, Lord, to Thee;
Take my moments and my days,
Let them flow in ceaseless praise.
(Frances Havergal, 1836–79)

SALLY WELCH

Dwelling on the past – or looking to the future?

Thus says the Lord, who makes a way in the sea, a path in the mighty waters... Do not remember the former things, or consider the things of old. I am about to do a new thing; now it springs forth; do you not perceive it? I will make a way in the wilderness and rivers in the desert. The wild animals will honour me, the jackals and the ostriches; for I give water in the wilderness, rivers in the desert, to give drink to my chosen people, the people whom I formed for myself so that they may proclaim my praise.

Recently I read in a newspaper about a village that was in uproar against its church because it had been decided to remove the Victorian pews in the nave and replace them with chairs. Perhaps the villagers felt that the building should remain as it was so that their memories could stay intact, a space preserved so that future rites of passage could resemble the ones of former times. Perhaps they needed the church as a symbol of stability in a constantly changing world – this took place during peak coronavirus time, when all around seemed dangerous and chaotic.

But change is part of the human experience – only God is constant. For every generation there must be a different way of speaking God's eternal truths into lives that are in need of the grace, forgiveness and love that only God can provide. So we are told not to dwell on the past, but to witness the new thing that God is doing in our midst – to witness, then to participate in the redemptive action of God.

What was previously barren desert will become fertile land, because God will provide the water of life for his people. And always we can look to God – in whom past, present and future are held in the certainty of love.

Oh, the future lies before me,
And I know not where I'll be;
But where'er my path be leading,
Saviour, keep my heart with Thee
(Jennie Stout, 1901).

SALLY WELCH

Eating together

Across the world, eating with other people is as natural as breathing. As the daughter of parents born and brought up in India, I was used to meals around the table including whoever was in the house at the time. I still recall with astonishment arriving at the home of a friend and being invited to wait in the sitting room while the family finished their meal.

There is something fundamental about sharing food with others; going beyond the basic need for fuel to remain active. Several cultures take hospitality so seriously that the immediate family might sacrifice their own food so that the guest will be fed. Perhaps this is hardly a surprise given that humans are created in the image of a generous, hospitable God: Creator, Son and Holy Spirit together forever. The Bible is crammed with stories involving food. Much of Jesus' ministry involved eating with other people. We read how the earliest Christians had to discover how, what, when and with whom they should eat. Eternally with God, heaven is depicted as a banquet. Eating together allows us to learn and practise Christian disciplines of hospitality, generosity and obedience though ritual and celebration.

Yet if eating together is profoundly human, what makes it a holy habit? We were created to acknowledge and depend on God's provision with thankfulness, but sin seems to have destroyed this basic God-given instinct. Sadly, throughout history the church has been (and still can be) exclusive rather than generous and hospitable; fearful and self-reliant rather than holy; power-seeking rather than vulnerable.

'Gluttony' is not a fashionable word, but it describes the eating habits of many of us, with obesity also found in those who rely on convenience food with high calorie content and low nutritional value. Drunkenness, destruction of God's creation by greedy people, eating disorders, starvation and food waste all indicate the need to seek God's way through.

The following studies emerged during the lockdowns due to Covid-19. Eating together for many people became restricted to those within the household, unless 'virtual' meals were shared using technology. As I write this, I am increasingly aware of God's gift of eating with others and pray that Christians will never take for granted the privilege of this holy habit.

LAKSHMI JEFFREYS

A shaky start

[Isaac] called his elder son Esau and said to him, 'My son'; and he answered, 'Here I am.' He said, 'See, I am old; I do not know the day of my death. Now then, take your weapons, your quiver and your bow, and go out to the field, and hunt game for me. Then prepare for me savoury food, such as I like, and bring it to me to eat, so that I may bless you before I die.'

The ritual of sharing a special meal is sacred, regardless of religious conviction. One of my favourite films is *Some Like It Hot*. Made in 1951 and set in the 1920s, it opens with gangsters infiltrating the birthday party of a rival criminal leader. The baddies emerge from an enormous birthday cake and gun down everyone in sight. The film really is a comedy, but this opening sequence exemplifies the horror of violating such an occasion.

While no one is murdered in the stories of Isaac, Esau and Jacob, there is profound abuse of ritual where food is involved. Esau sells his birthright (the entitlement to become the head of the household) to Jacob for a bowl of stew (Genesis 25:29–34). Following today's reading, Jacob and his mother trick Isaac into blessing Jacob rather than his older brother as they give the blind old man his favourite meal.

Despite Jacob's deceit, Esau's appetite and Isaac's attempt to circumvent the prophecy that the older brother would serve the younger (Genesis 25), God's plan for the salvation of humanity is furthered through Jacob stealing Esau's birthright. As a descendant of Abraham, not only would Jacob inherit a double portion of his father's property, he would be the one through whom God's covenant blessing would be given.

Christians perhaps can take comfort from God's plan being fulfilled regardless of human self-will and disobedience. At the same time, it is worth pausing to reflect on how sometimes we take lightly meals with other people that they might consider significant. What might happen if we remembered God can work through every occasion we eat with other people?

Teach us to listen well to you and to our companions
when eating with others.

LAKSHMI JEFFREYS

Accommodating difference

They served [Joseph] by himself, and them by themselves, and the Egyptians who ate with him by themselves, because the Egyptians could not eat with the Hebrews, for that is an abomination to the Egyptians. When they were seated before him, the firstborn according to his birthright and the youngest according to his youth, the men looked at one another in amazement. Portions were taken to them from Joseph's table, but Benjamin's portion was five times as much as any of theirs.

Today's reading appears to demonstrate further flagrant disregard of birthright. While the brothers are seated in order of seniority, the youngest receives so much more food than anyone else. And during such a significant meal, the host sits apart. Technicoloured dreamcoat in the distant past, Joseph has assimilated into Egyptian culture. Unwilling to reveal his true identity, he follows the customs of the country, feigning distaste for the people of God. (The actual reason is not known; perhaps the ancient Egyptians had various animals they considered sacred and these might have been at odds with Hebrew practice.) By the end of the story, Pharaoh is so impressed with Joseph that he welcomes Jacob's whole family. Furthermore, the Egyptian leader accommodates the Hebrews to enable them to thrive as God's people.

Years ago friends of mine worked with a mission agency in a cosmopolitan city in India where Christians, Hindus, Muslims, Sikhs, Jains and others lived alongside one another. Socialising always involved food but was often limited according to various religious dietary restrictions. When I visited them, my friends explained that not only would we eat vegetarian meals, but they would not buy any animal products, as they had become friendly with a Jain family who would not cross the threshold if there was any meat in the house. My friends took seriously the need to share the gospel in their particular setting. My friends' respect for their neighbours fascinated the head of the Jain household; he sought to learn more about the God whose followers were so clear in their faith, yet generous in how they related to others.

Do you thank God before every meal, regardless of who is with you?

LAKSHMI JEFFREYS

Sacramental dining

Moses and Aaron, Nadab, and Abihu, and seventy of the elders of Israel went up, and they saw the God of Israel. Under his feet there was something like a pavement of sapphire stone, like the very heaven for clearness. God did not lay his hand on the chief men of the people of Israel; also they beheld God, and they ate and drank. The Lord said to Moses, 'Come up to me on the mountain, and wait there; and I will give you the tablets of stone, with the law and the commandment... for their instruction.'

After centuries of slavery in Egypt, God's people are discovering what it means to have been chosen by God. They are thankful immediately after God acts dramatically in their favour. Sadly, within a short time they return to grumbling and forget God's love for them. While there are countless occasions on which God's people are disobedient in the wilderness, today's passage offers an unusual glimpse of an early sacramental meal.

A sacrament is a visible sign of God's unseen reality. Christian denominations differ over what they consider formal sacraments. Within the Anglican Church, the sacraments are baptism and Holy Communion: outward signs of the Holy Spirit transforming the community following Jesus' death and resurrection. Sacraments, special times of God with people, strengthen the people for their next step on the journey. God remains totally other and intimately present in any sacrament.

Here is a picture of what it means to have God with God's people. Up to this point the Lord has appeared so holy and unapproachable that even to touch the mountain on which God meets Moses leads to death. God speaks of his majesty and power and their relative insignificance. Yet here are the leaders of God's people with God, enjoying not the manna collected on a daily basis but fine dining. The unapproachable God is with them.

Noteworthy meals for birthdays or weddings mark the beginning of a new stage of life: the next year for an individual or the lifelong partnership of a couple. Can you imagine how these occasions can become sacramental when we explicitly remember that God is with us?

Thank you, God, for your delight to celebrate with us
as we embark on the next step.

LAKSHMI JEFFREYS

True holiness

For the Lord your God is God of gods and Lord of lords, the great God, mighty and awesome, who is not partial and takes no bribe, who executes justice for the orphan and the widow, and who loves the strangers, providing them with food and clothing. You shall also love the stranger, for you were strangers in the land of Egypt. You shall fear the Lord your God; him alone you shall worship; to him you shall hold fast, and by his name you shall swear.

Yesterday we encountered the majestic God having an intimate and joyful meal with the leaders of the people. Today we are offered instruction on how to emulate God's holiness. In Moses' time and still today, the most revered people in society were those who demonstrated their wealth, power or status. Rulers met with other rulers: ordinary children, women and men existed simply to do their bidding and were not dining companions.

Holiness implies 'otherness'. Yet the God who is most powerful and holy shows no partiality for riches, rank or other human concerns. This God asks the same of his people. The paradox is that if we are to be truly holy and 'other', we need to share ourselves and our table with anyone and everyone, not simply people who are like us. Jesus frequently dined with people whom the religious authorities avoided. He demonstrated that true holiness comes not from following regulations but from transformation by the God whose love cannot be tainted by any person, object or situation.

Sharing meals regularly with people with whom we would not naturally socialise is demanding. A young couple would hear the doorbell as they were preparing their evening meal: the visitor had mental health issues but would sit down to dine with them. A woman in her 90s prepares 'homeless sandwiches' every two weeks for a local soup kitchen. A family who worked at the drop-in centre offered a fine-dining experience every month to one of the clients. Each host was aware of the personal (and financial) cost but also of blessing outweighing the sense of duty.

Loving God, help me to see myself and others
as equally created in your image.

LAKSHMI JEFFREYS

Emotional eating

Then Jonathan answered his father Saul, 'Why should he be put to death? What has he done?' But Saul threw his spear at him to strike him; so Jonathan knew that it was the decision of his father to put David to death. Jonathan rose from the table in fierce anger and ate no food on the second day of the month, for he was grieved for David, and because his father had disgraced him.

Eating is so much more than refuelling the body. We speak about 'feeling' hungry. A gory story takes away appetite: we might require nourishment, but the horrible image in our mind overrides basic hunger pangs. Eating alone in an environment where everyone else seems to be in company feels uncomfortable, no matter how much we like the food before us. Most importantly, there are people whose mental ill health is demonstrated by an inability to eat, particularly when other people are around.

Eating with other people always involves emotions. Sharing food is an intimate experience. The stranger on the train who offered me a crisp immediately became a travelling companion (*com* = with; *pan* = bread) even without extensive conversation. Simply eating a salty snack with someone else elicited thankfulness and delight.

In the reading, on the other hand, Saul's jealousy of David and ultimatum to Jonathan to give up his friendship with David or ruin the family leads to a complete breakdown in the relationship between father and son. Jonathan finds it impossible to eat with the man who has effectively destroyed the bond between them. I have seen people leave food and drink in a pub when someone has arrived against whom they bore a grudge. It is deeply sad.

Jesus' life, death and resurrection restored our relationship with God, with one another and with ourselves. We do well to recognise that our spiritual, emotional, social, physical and mental well-being are intrinsically linked. While improving our diet can aid our mental health, perhaps as we receive and offer God's forgiveness, our entire well-being will benefit.

Pray for everyone struggling with or researching mental health and eating disorders.

LAKSHMI JEFFREYS

Celebration in context

All the rest of Israel were of a single mind to make David king. They were there with David for three days, eating and drinking, for their kindred had provided for them. And also their neighbours, from as far away as Issachar and Zebulun and Naphtali, came bringing food on donkeys, camels, mules, and oxen – abundant provisions of meal, cakes of figs, clusters of raisins, wine, oil, oxen, and sheep, for there was joy in Israel.

Saul is dead and God's people remain at war with the Philistines. Sadly, they are divided: some wish to remain loyal to the family of the former monarch, while many others, including members of Saul's own tribe of Benjamin, have elected to follow David. The verses preceding today's reading detail the range of people who recognise David as God's chosen leader. Their families provide food, and the feast is enjoyed for days. David and the tribal leaders then search out the ark of the covenant so that they can discover God's will (1 Chronicles 13).

It is important not to allow circumstances to thwart valid celebration. (We shall see in a subsequent reading God's response to inappropriate celebration.) I know a couple who married during the coronavirus pandemic. Their wedding was not as they had imagined it would be, but their joy at sharing the wedding meal with immediate family was evident. In years to come, they will have big parties with friends and others. On their wedding day they were able to focus on what was important: their commitment before God to live together in love and faithfulness. Their intimate reception meal was a beautiful celebration of this.

Western society often suggests that consuming lavish food in extravagant settings is essential to commemorate a special occasion. Some of the wedding receptions I have enjoyed most belie this. Here the food was provided by members of the church, who also decorated the venue and served the many guests. There is a powerful sense of Jesus' presence when Christians provide food to bless other people. This is the case when church members host a monthly shared lunch or provide free coffee and home-baked goods after a service.

Jesus promises to be with those who gather in his name (Matthew 18:20).

LAKSHMI JEFFREYS

Feeding the enemy

When the king of Israel saw them he said to Elisha, 'Father, shall I kill them? Shall I kill them?' He answered, 'No! Did you capture with your sword and your bow those whom you want to kill? Set food and water before them so that they may eat and drink; and let them go to their master.' So he prepared for them a great feast; after they ate and drank, he sent them on their way, and they went to their master. And the Arameans no longer came raiding into the land of Israel.

Elisha is God's prophet while God's people Israel are at war with the Arameans. The previous verses chronicle various miracles God performs through Elisha, including causing the enemy soldiers to become blind. Elisha then guides the sightless men into the camp of the king of Israel. What follows is an indication that the most effective way to destroy an enemy is to make them a friend.

There are themes of spiritual blindness and sight to the things of God. In addition, today's story puts into practice Proverbs 25:21–22: feeding the hungry enemy, thereby heaping burning coals on their head and being rewarded by God. Paul quotes these verses when offering various examples of love in Romans 12. Once again Christians are invited to demonstrate God's ways rather than to instinctively retaliate.

Providing nourishment for someone who is hostile or afraid can be utterly disarming. Various areas of conflict have been managed effectively over a coffee and a piece of cake at a neutral venue, as I have allowed myself to be vulnerable in conversation and generous in providing food. In one case, an individual did anything they could to avoid me; then we ate and drank together and discovered God's grace and the means to end the dispute. On another occasion, an atheist and his wife came for a meal at the rectory. He was terrified at what he might encounter, but at the end of a delightful evening we began what has become a close family friendship.

'You prepare a table before… my enemies' (Psalm 23:5).
Does David feast with his enemies? Does God provide for David
in front of them? What is the effect on the enemies?

LAKSHMI JEFFREYS

Inappropriate celebration

On that day the Lord God of hosts called to weeping and mourning, to baldness and putting on sackcloth; but instead there was joy and festivity, killing oxen and slaughtering sheep, eating meat and drinking wine. 'Let us eat and drink, for tomorrow we die.' The Lord of hosts has revealed himself in my ears: Surely this iniquity will not be forgiven you until you die, says the Lord God of hosts.

As indicated in the introduction, at the time of writing the world is in the grip of the coronavirus pandemic. Meanwhile other countries in the world are ravaged by combinations of the disease, famine and war.

At the beginning of the outbreak in this country, supermarket shelves were stripped of much food and other household goods. Queues were seen reminiscent of those during wartime rationing. Recipes for cheap, nutritious meals flooded all forms of media, and there was genuine concern for housebound people and others who would not be able to buy food. Yet only a few weeks later, as pubs and restaurants opened amid desperation to kick-start the economy, the atmosphere changed. Many individuals returned to a desire to live well on their terms. Apparently, they forgot lessons learned earlier in the year concerning care for others and reflection on how human folly contributed to the mess.

Will we ever learn? Isaiah was challenging God's people about the same matters in a completely different context. Jerusalem had escaped attack from an enemy, so there was rejoicing. They totally ignored the present reality of suffering among their own people in other areas. Their extravagant feasting was utterly inappropriate and left no space to listen to God.

After a time of trial, it is important to celebrate but only in the context of thankfulness to God. This is not the excessive gorging challenged by Isaiah. There will have been time to reflect and, where necessary, to repent. Subsequent feasting will acknowledge and hold before God those still suffering. There will be a desire for everyone to enjoy God's freedom and hope.

Complacency is never godly (Luke 12:17–20)

LAKSHMI JEFFREYS

Religious celebration?

Rural Jews… observe… a day of joy and feasting… Mordecai recorded these events, and he sent letters to all the Jews… that they should celebrate annually… the time when the Jews got relief from their enemies, and as the month when their sorrow was turned into joy and their mourning into a day of celebration. He wrote to them to observe the days as days of feasting and joy and giving presents of food to one another and gifts to the poor.

God is not mentioned throughout the book of Esther, whose primary purpose is to provide a basis for the Jewish festival Purim. Jewish settlers in Persia have been persecuted, but Esther (married to the Persian king) and Mordecai save their people from annihilation by the Persians. The king allows the Jews to put to death the main villain, Haman, his family and supporters. Mordecai and Esther then give instructions about when and how two days of festivities should take place. The story of Jewish persecution but ultimate triumph is to be remembered every year by every generation.

With its colourful costumes and wonderful food, Purim is enjoyed by many regardless of religious faith. There are similarities with Christmas celebrations across the world: many people know little of the story, seeking instead an opportunity for food, drink and merriment; the poor are remembered, but there might be no awareness of Jesus at the centre of events.

In the story of Esther, the queen fasts before she risks divulging her Jewish heritage and the plot against her people. The period of fasting and reflection gives way to feasting at the appropriate time. In the Christian calendar, Advent precedes Christmas. Yet many churches barely pay lip service to the weeks of preparation, instead, seemingly out of nowhere, throwing a lavish birthday party for Jesus.

Purim has an advantage over Christmas in that the story is told in detail in the Bible. The events leading to the birth of Jesus in the Bible need to be pieced together from different accounts. It is easy to focus on innkeepers, donkeys and other characters not present in the text and lose sight of God's Son and the purpose of remembering and celebrating.

The birth of Jesus is for life, not just for Christmas!

LAKSHMI JEFFREYS

To eat or not to eat...?

But Daniel resolved that he would not defile himself with the royal rations of food and wine; so he asked the palace master to allow him not to defile himself.

If an unbeliever invites you to a meal... eat whatever is set before you without raising any question on the ground of conscience. But if someone says to you, 'This has been offered in sacrifice', then do not eat it... So, whether you eat or drink, or whatever you do, do everything for the glory of God.

In the west, many Christians have the luxury of making lifestyle choices with food. Friends who are vegetarian or vegan will quote Bible passages to strengthen their argument for not eating meat. Of course, some people need to avoid certain food for medical reasons. In the next study, we shall explore the importance of accepting hospitality and how that affects what we eat. Today, however, the focus is on another aspect of Christian witness.

Daniel has been taken from Jerusalem and is in the court of King Nebuchadnezzar in Babylon. With nothing around him to enable him to live as one of God's people, Daniel elects to maintain the food laws handed down from Moses: he rejects what he is given from the king's table, and God blesses him. The apostle Paul, on the other hand, is writing to Christians in a cosmopolitan city where all sorts of religious worship takes place. Food from the market has been offered in worship to idols. The living God takes a dim view of idolatry; Paul invites his readers to make decisions 'on the ground of conscience'.

Having converted from a Hindu background, for me this was a personal issue. A Hindu priest would place food in worship before idols in the house; this food would later become the main meal. I wanted both to take a stand as a Christian and to show respect to my family. For a number of months, I had genuine reasons not to be around when the ceremonies were taking place. With a desire to respect my family, I resolved not to eat certain items which had special religious significance but to enjoy the rest.

May Christians eat with people of other faiths for the glory of God.

LAKSHMI JEFFREYS

Receiving hospitality

If anyone is there who shares in peace, your peace will rest on that person; but if not, it will return to you. Remain in the same house, eating and drinking whatever they provide, for the labourer deserves to be paid. Do not move about from house to house. Whenever you enter a town and its people welcome you, eat what is set before you; cure the sick who are there, and say to them, 'The kingdom of God has come near to you.'

Yesterday we explored demonstrating Christian faith when eating with people who might not share this. Today's reading involves hospitality with those sympathetic to faith.

Several years ago, at the beginning of the coldest December on record where we lived, our boiler exploded. We had to heat water in a kettle or on the stove for washing and after a disaster involving our young son, neighbours kindly allowed us to use their baths and showers. While enormously grateful, I am ashamed to say it did not take us long to rank the bathrooms in order of our preference.

Jesus has sent out 70 of his disciples to prepare local villages for a visit from Jesus. He instructs his followers to accept hospitality when offered and not to compare one household with another. After all, the householders are persons of peace: those who wish to support the workers in their endeavours for the kingdom. While the food they provide might not be what the disciples prefer, it would be sustaining and offered with love. (My taste for fresh ground coffee does not allow me to be snobbish and refuse the hospitality of a person who provides instant coffee.) While proclaiming the kingdom in word and deed, the disciples are also learning utterly to depend on God's provision. Accepting hospitality with thankfulness is part of their remarkable witness.

We are called by Jesus to share the kingdom of God. Genuine gratitude and vulnerability are in short supply in the world. How we behave when receiving hospitality is as important as being willing to offer hospitality and says something about God, who became utterly dependent on others.

Allow Philippians 2:5–8 to inform your attitude as a guest

LAKSHMI JEFFREYS

Love your neighbour

Let love be genuine; hate what is evil, hold fast to what is good; love one another with mutual affection; outdo one another in showing honour. Do not lag in zeal, be ardent in spirit, serve the Lord... Contribute to the needs of the saints; extend hospitality to strangers... If it is possible, so far as it depends on you, live peaceably with all... 'If your enemies are hungry, feed them; if they are thirsty, give them something to drink; for by doing this you will heap burning coals on their heads.'

Leaving aside the heaping of burning coals on the heads of our enemies (see 2 October), this passage from Paul's letter to Christians in Rome gives us pictures of what love looks like. God's love is for members of the household of faith and those beyond – and it is completely practical. Feeding and watering strangers and our enemies comes more naturally to some people than to others, but it is a command to all Christian communities.

At the beginning of lockdown, when all social contact beyond the immediate household was forbidden, people were ingenious in finding ways to eat with friends, family and neighbours. As well as 'Zoom parties' (other platforms are available), people with gardens invited others living in flats or places without outdoor space to bring something to eat and drink so they could have a meal together. The most heartening sight was of householders sitting in front of their dwellings on a Saturday or Sunday afternoon enjoying afternoon tea together. So many church members commented that they had lived in their house for a number of years, but it was only now that they were getting to know their neighbours.

It need not take a global pandemic to encourage Christians to eat with their neighbours. If we are zealous in our love for God and other people but cooking is not our thing or we don't feel able to open our homes, there is much we can do to offer hospitality. A friend was deserted by her husband and left alone in a large house. Although she hated the property, she recognised it as God's gift and lent it to the church for social events.

How can you offer hospitality?

LAKSHMI JEFFREYS

God's way

Then the king will say to those at his right hand, 'Come, you that are blessed by my Father, inherit the kingdom prepared for you from the foundation of the world; for I was hungry and you gave me food, I was thirsty and you gave me something to drink, I was a stranger and you welcomed me, I was naked and you gave me clothing, I was sick and you took care of me, I was in prison and you visited me.'

Jesus' parable about God's judgement is clear. Those who feed the hungry, whoever they are, God will bless. Those who fail to act – not necessarily doing the wrong thing but failing to be compassionate – God will condemn. There is debate about whether the recipients of kindness in the parable are members of the household of faith. Whatever the case, maybe the Christian community is a good place to start. There are many organisations working with churches across the world where people are starving.

What has this to do with the holy habit of eating together? I heard on the news recently in the UK that food banks are in greater demand than ever. At the same time, we are bombarded with statistics about obesity, especially among children and young people, many of whom develop deficiency disorders. Add to this a world food crisis due to, among other things, conflict, human greed, climate crisis and natural disasters, all exacerbated by a global pandemic, and suddenly I am more aware of what I eat, with whom and where it comes from.

In Acts the church is seen to be a community that shared food together regularly with great joy, so that there was no poor person among them. This is a picture of God's kingdom in practice, which we will experience fully in heaven. In scripture heaven is depicted as a wonderful banquet (Isaiah 25:6–9); meanwhile only those who accept the host's invitation, however unlikely, will partake (Luke 14:15–24). In this case we need to practise being alert to God's voice and sharing food with those immediately around us and beyond. How might you or your church respond?

Loving God, have mercy on our world of plenty where millions are hungry; our world of many where millions are lonely.

LAKSHMI JEFFREYS

Transformation

But they urged him strongly, saying, 'Stay with us, because it is almost evening and the day is now nearly over.' So he went in to stay with them. When he was at the table with them, he took bread, blessed and broke it, and gave it to them. Then their eyes were opened, and they recognised him; and he vanished from their sight. They said to each other, 'Were not our hearts burning within us while he was talking to us on the road, while he was opening the scriptures to us?'

The story of the risen Jesus meeting Cleopas and another dejected disciple on the Emmaus road exudes beauty, humour and, above all, real hope. As the disciples tell their sad tale they utter the poignant phrase 'We had hoped' (Luke 24:21). The combination of scripture, Christian fellowship and breaking bread enables Jesus' followers to discover that he has been with them. By the time the risen Christ disappears, Cleopas and his friend have been heard and blessed by him. They recognise their hopes have been realised but in ways they could never have imagined, and they rush off to tell their friends. The account ends as they tell an astonished Peter and the others that the Lord was made know to them 'in the breaking of bread' (24:35).

Naturally any action, including sharing food, is made holy by God. Without wanting to over-spiritualise the Emmaus road encounter, the act of Jesus breaking bread evokes much, including the Last Supper and, for many Christians, Holy Communion. For me, the importance of developing holy habits as a body of believers cannot be overstated. As we regularly share meals with others within and beyond the church, we can become alert to prompting by the Holy Spirit as we speak, eat and drink with other people. Combine this awareness with the study of scripture, and we shall know when to talk overtly about Jesus and when to allow our actions and attitudes to speak for us. My prayer is for you to discover, within and beyond your church, how God is inviting you to eat with others, individually and as a body of believers.

Transform our attitudes and actions, Holy Spirit, as we eat together.

LAKSHMI JEFFREYS

Psalms 57—70: 'All human life is there'

As we get older, my wife and I are intrigued at the perception our grandchildren have of their grandparents. We'd like to think they see us as wise and full of fun – the truth, in other words. We suspect they see us as dedicated cheapskates, willing to scour the Saturday car boot sale seeking out bargains on their behalf and always ready with a coupon for a cut-price meal out.

We know that we have one talent they regard with an irritated fascination – the ability and willingness to come up with a song for every occasion. Fascination, in that we never let them down: a passing remark, a road sign, a friend's name – to their amazement all seem able to trigger a burst of not very tuneful warbling. Irritation, because they never know the song and it interrupts the flow of the conversation.

The Psalms offer a song for every occasion. There is an extraordinary breadth of content and emotion. There are words written by a man on the run in fear of his life; an abuser of power full of remorse; one whose friends have abandoned him; a shepherd, a warrior, a king; full of life, fearful of death; triumphant, then deeply ashamed; a father losing his child, betrayed by his sons; full of friendship, anger, despair, joy and trust.

All human life is there – and unlike the now defunct Sunday paper that was sold under that slogan (*News of the World*), they still offer thoughtful reading and uplifting content.

The Psalms are far more than cleverly constructed literary masterpieces, more than words enhanced by the mysterious beauty of plainsong. They are a revelation, created by human beings wrestling with their relationship with God amid all the complexities of life, discovering what the world is like and how God interacts with that reality.

As we sample just 14 of these nuggets of spiritual insight over the next two weeks, my hope and prayer is that you will find the words, the thought, the emotion, the experience – something that links you into the world of the psalmist in which daily reality, with all its highs and lows, is suffused with the worship of almighty God.

STEPHEN RAND

Mercy and music

Have mercy on me, my God… I am in the midst of lions; I am forced to dwell among ravenous beasts – men whose teeth are spears and arrows, whose tongues are sharp swords. Be exalted, O God, above the heavens; let your glory be over all the earth. They spread a net for my feet – I was bowed down in distress. They dug a pit in my path – but they have fallen into it themselves. My heart, O God, is steadfast, my heart is steadfast; I will sing and make music.

The heading to this psalm explains its context: 'When David had fled from Saul into the cave.' King Saul had collected a posse of 3,000 men to hunt David down (1 Samuel 24). They were like 'ravenous beasts'; he was in 'the midst of lions', running for his life. No wonder the psalm begins 'Have mercy on me.'

The heading also describes the psalm as a *miktam*; the meaning of this Hebrew word is unclear, but I like the possibility that it is 'a silent prayer'. David is in darkness at the back of the cave; the entrance is blocked by Saul and his men. David cries out for mercy – very quietly, for fear of discovery. But God can hear our whispers, our silent prayers.

David is not concerned simply for his own safety, looking to God for salvation. The psalm bounces between graphic descriptions of the dangers that surround him and outbursts of worship: his enemies dug a pit; his God is exalted over all the earth. That gives him the confidence not only to trust God ('my heart is steadfast') but to look forward to bursting into song when the time for the silent prayer is over.

The God we cry out to for mercy when we are overwhelmed is the one whose glory is over all the earth. It's easy for stresses and strains to restrict our view of God, but holding on to a vision of the reality of his greatness and his global reach will give us the confidence to trust him. Even when I am backed into the darkness of a cave, I can never escape his presence. He sees me; he is with me.

Heavenly Father, when there seems to be no escape,
hear my cry for mercy and enable me to sing your praise. Amen

STEPHEN RAND

The judge of all the earth

Do you rulers indeed speak justly? Do you judge people with equity? No, in your heart you devise injustice, and your hands mete out violence on the earth… The righteous will be glad when they are avenged, when they dip their feet in the blood of the wicked. Then people will say, 'Surely the righteous still are rewarded; surely there is a God who judges the earth.'

Today I read about a judge who ruled that a 14-year-old Christian girl who had been kidnapped, forced to convert and made to marry a man who already had a wife should be taken from her place of refuge and returned to her abductor.

How angry are we when faced with injustice? I am furious when I am on the receiving end. My wife never ceases to be amused that I still remember the day when I was unjustly punished at school – I was six. (She thinks the song for this occasion is probably 'Let It Go'!)

But how much do I care when people I don't know suffer at the hands of corrupt judges and power-hungry rulers? I can scarcely claim that I don't know – it is a regular feature of our news media. But it is all too easy to enjoy my own safety and security and suppress the concern that I might feel.

David sees himself as the victim of injustice and appears to look for bloodthirsty vengeance. We rightly reject revenge, but do we look for righteousness? I once read of a man who lived surrounded by poverty and injustice. He investigated the great religions of the world, then opted to become a Christian. Why? Because Christianity was, in his view, the only religion that promised judgement on those who meted out injustice and oppression.

I've been encouraging God's people to be true to God's word and take action for justice for over 40 years. I still think it matters to write to my MP and raise my voice on behalf of those who have no voice. It matters because justice matters. And, praise God, sometimes it makes a difference.

God of justice, I pray for justice. And help me to be part of the answer to my prayer.

STEPHEN RAND

My refuge in times of trouble

Deliver me from my enemies, O God; be my fortress against those who are attacking me. Deliver me from evildoers and save me from those who are after my blood… But I will sing of your strength, in the morning I will sing of your love; for you are my fortress, my refuge in times of trouble. You are my strength, I sing praise to you; you, God, are my fortress, my God on whom I can rely.

This psalm's introduction says 'When Saul had sent men to watch David's house in order to kill him.' That certainly explains the first line! Once again David is under threat, surrounded by enemies. Once again he is looking for deliverance.

The heading also includes these words: 'To the tune of "Do Not Destroy".' Leaving aside the fascination that 3,000 years after it was written we can still know the name of the tune (with no idea of how that tune sounded), why this name? Was it because the theme of the psalm was David's plea for deliverance? Or is there a subtler meaning? Part of the story of Saul's pursuit of David is that there is a moment when Saul is at David's mercy in the cave, and David's instruction to his men is, 'Do not destroy.'

There's an echo here of a basic truth, encapsulated in the Lord's Prayer: 'Forgive us our sins, as we forgive those who sin against us.' The very things we want God to do for us, we have to be prepared to do for others.

David begins his prayer by calling out to God to be his fortress and his refuge. He ends his prayer by singing out that God *is* his fortress and his refuge. In our prayers, there is no point in asking God to be something that he is not, but there is every point in asking God to be to us something that we know him to be. Why? Because he is faithful; he can be relied on.

David sets his words of confident praise in the context of God's love: the word 'love' is often translated in the King James Version as 'lovingkindness'. David was confident of his prayer being answered because he was confident of God's lovingkindness.

Be assured and reassured: God loves you.

STEPHEN RAND

Desperate times

You have rejected us, God, and burst upon us; you have been angry – now restore us! You have shaken the land and torn it open; mend its fractures, for it is quaking. You have shown your people desperate times; you have given us wine that makes us stagger. But for those who fear you, you have raised a banner to be unfurled against the bow. Save us and help us with your right hand, that those you love may be delivered.

This is King David. God has seen him through his battles with Saul; now he is winning battles and extending his power and influence. Then comes a crushing defeat. David does not see it as a military setback. Rather he perceives something deeper, even more terrifying: God has rejected his people. David uses the language of catastrophe. He feels like he has been hit by an earthquake; he is staggered at the reversal. The land, God's great gift to his people, has been torn open. The times are desperate.

Does any of this strike a chord? A time when your world was turned upside down? It was all going so well, then suddenly… disaster.

I am not sure, on the basis of the nature of God revealed in the Bible, that God actually rejects us. I do not believe that calamity is sent from him as an angry sideswipe or to teach us a lesson (though we can certainly learn lessons in catastrophe that we cannot learn any other way). But I am sure that there are times when it certainly feels as though God has rejected and abandoned us. We can find ourselves crying out, 'My God, my God, why have you forsaken me?' (Psalm 22:1).

That's how David felt. But he held on to the truth that we highlighted yesterday: he was still loved by God. That's why he clings on to God through the storm; he ends the psalm declaring 'With God we shall gain the victory' (v. 12).

It's easy for me to write that, even after the darkest hour, the dawn will come. I'm under no illusion, however, that when you are in the midst of the darkness, this is less easy to believe.

God has said, 'Never will I leave you; never will I forsake you'
(Hebrews 13:5).

STEPHEN RAND

Journey into life

Hear my cry, O God; listen to my prayer. From the ends of the earth I call to you, I call as my heart grows faint; lead me to the rock that is higher than I. For you have been my refuge, a strong tower against the foe. I long to dwell in your tent for ever and take refuge in the shelter of your wings. For you, God, have heard my vows; you have given me the heritage of those who fear your name.

Come and join me on the psalmist's journey. It begins at the 'ends of the earth'. Far from the temple, the place where God lived, as far away as it was possible to be. This may have been a geographical reality. I have been to places that seemed impossibly remote, such as deep in the Honduran rainforest or among the windswept mists at Cape Horn. But however far from home we may be, nowhere is remote to God. We can be sure he hears our cry.

Perhaps it was more a spiritual reality. The writer's heart is growing faint; he feels he is far from God. He is sending out a distress call: he wants a beacon to guide him to the rock. Some commentators think this is a reference to the Temple Mount in Jerusalem, others that it is simply a description of God. The word is literally the 'cliffs', a place where from the top you can look down, safe from the pounding waves below. Somewhere solid, somewhere (someone) strong, the very opposite of the faint-hearted.

The rock is the basis of a refuge, a strong tower – a place of security, thick walls and heavy gates. But having reached safety and sanctuary, there is a new longing and a new destination – 'to dwell in the tent'. The tent was where God lived. It was the place of warmth, fellowship and hospitality. It was where the opportunity would come to be so close that it would be just like a tiny chick snuggled up to its mother, under the shelter of her wings. Nothing could be closer, nothing more tender.

Thank you, Almighty God, that you made me for the closest possible relationship with you. Help me to get closer, day by day.

STEPHEN RAND

The choice is yours

Truly he is my rock and my salvation; he is my fortress, I shall not be shaken. My salvation and my honour depend on God; he is my mighty rock, my refuge. Trust in him at all times, you people; pour out your hearts to him, for God is our refuge. Surely the lowborn are but a breath, the highborn are but a lie. If weighed on a balance, they are nothing; together they are only a breath. Do not trust in extortion or put vain hope in stolen goods; though your riches increase, do not set your heart on them. One thing God has spoken, two things I have heard: 'Power belongs to you, God, and with you, Lord, is unfailing love'; and, 'You reward everyone according to what they have done.'

David is convinced. His experience of life, and of God, leads him to a repeated refrain, like the chorus in an old hymn: God can be trusted.

God is his rest, his rock, his refuge, his salvation. All the glory and honour given to David are rightly due to God. He is unshakeable in believing this; because he believes this, he is unshakeable.

So he wants his people to make the same choice, the same commitment to God ('Trust in him at all times'), not just with their heads, but also with their hearts ('Pour out your hearts to him'). When a priest made a sacrifice, the blood was 'poured out'. David wanted them to share their whole lives, their innermost thoughts, their deepest longings. *The Message* paraphrase says, 'Lay your lives on the line for him'.

What are the alternatives? Other people? They are just a breath, a vanity, a vapour – unreliable, here today and gone tomorrow. Money? It's a 'vain hope'. God offers something very different: not only his power and strength, but his 'unfailing love'.

The choice David offered his people is one we have to make. And it matters, because God will 'reward' you according to your decision. 'Reward' may not be the best translation – that last phrase could be rendered: 'God will make his peace with you if you choose to trust him.'

Father, help me today to opt for your unfailing love and to trust you with my life.

STEPHEN RAND

The God of relationship

You, God, are my God, earnestly I seek you; I thirst for you, my whole being longs for you, in a dry and parched land where there is no water. I have seen you in the sanctuary and beheld your power and your glory. Because your love is better than life, my lips will glorify you. I will praise you as long as I live, and in your name I will lift up my hands.

The heading for this psalm is terse: 'A psalm of David. When he was in the Desert of Judah.' This may relate to the time when his son Absalom rebelled and chased David out into the desert. So at the very moment when he is most aware of the breakdown of a relationship within his own family, David writes a psalm that is deeply poignant, a heartfelt song of relationship.

It begins with a simple yet profound statement: 'You, God, are my God.' In the culture of the time everyone had their own personal god. It was one among many. There was no claim of superiority, no competition implied. You worship yours, I'll worship mine.

But the writer's claim here is very different, outrageous. God, the Almighty God, the only true and living God – he is my God. I belong to the king of all creation, and he belongs to me. We are in relationship. We walk together; we talk together. He hears and answers my prayers. Christianity is not about believing the right things and doing the best we can. It's about entering into and then living out a personal relationship with God – Father, Son and Holy Spirit.

It's so personal it is intimate. The psalmist uses the language of love – his whole being longs for God. He is in the desert, desperate for water. He is in a desert of broken relationships, and he thirsts for God.

I find this deeply challenging. How much do I seek God? How thirsty am I for his presence? Then I think of those I know of through my work with Open Doors, those who died a martyr's death, their lips glorifying God because for them God's love really was 'better than life'.

Help me to long for you and praise you for as long as I live.

STEPHEN RAND

God hears, God acts

Hear me, my God, as I voice my complaint; protect my life from the threat of the enemy. Hide me from the conspiracy of the wicked… They sharpen their tongues like swords and aim cruel words like deadly arrows… They plot injustice and say, 'We have devised a perfect plan!' Surely the human mind and heart are cunning. But God will shoot them with his arrows; they will suddenly be struck down. He will turn their own tongues against them and bring them to ruin; all who see them will shake their heads in scorn. All people will fear; they will proclaim the works of God and ponder what he has done.

This is one of the psalms that hints at having been written as liturgy, perhaps for use in the temple, rather than as a private prayer. It starts with an individual, not so much praying as laying down a challenge: the Hebrew words are most simply translated as 'God, hear my voice.' The psalmist is not complaining to or about God; he is summoning God to come and hear his formal complaint, his lawsuit, and make a judgement. His life is at stake; he is in need of protection from the conspiracy of the wicked.

Then it's as if the first witness is called. They describe the nature of the threat: its weapons are words, its method is cunning, the aim is injustice. This is unexpected. David lived in a world of violence: battles, betrayals, murder, mayhem. But we all live in a world where words can wound – 'cruel words like deadly arrows'. It can be true in our families, our church or our workplace. And the impact can be devastating: broken relationships, broken homes. The way words have been used in our civil and political life in recent years has left society, if not quite broken, certainly deeply scarred and wounded, with tragic evidence of injustice.

Then there is another voice: judgement is pronounced. God will intervene: their arrows will be turned against them, their words will be the source of their demise. Finally, a fourth voice announces that all will see what God has done, and they will ponder. In the end, justice is done. God always hears.

Lord, give me wisdom with my words.

STEPHEN RAND

God provides

You care for the land and water it; you enrich it abundantly. The streams of God are filled with water to provide the people with corn, for so you have ordained it. You drench its furrows and level its ridges; you soften it with showers and bless its crops. You crown the year with your bounty, and your carts overflow with abundance. The grasslands of the wilderness overflow; the hills are clothed with gladness. The meadows are covered with flocks and the valleys are mantled with corn; they shout for joy and sing.

I love harvest festivals. For many years at Tearfund I produced resources for use at harvest festival services. I was particularly proud of a family-service talk based on the story of God giving manna in the wilderness. The two key points of the talk were regularly repeated, and the congregation had to respond with the appropriate sound effect, so that 'God provides' was greeted with enthusiastic applause and 'Greed smells' with a corporate cry of 'Ew, pong!' while everyone held their nose.

Today's psalm certainly fulfils the main purpose of a harvest festival: reminding us that God provides all that we have and all that we need for life itself. But it goes much further. It stresses that God's provision comes from his care for the land. Concern for our environment is not a trendy green liberal fad; for a Christian it stems from the conviction that if God made the world and cares for it, so should we.

This is important enough, but there is an even deeper truth. These are not the only verses in the Bible that talk about the creation singing in worship to its creator. In one sense this can be seen as no more than poetic exuberance. It may be similarly poetic to suggest that during lockdown many people heard nature singing perhaps as never before.

The theological truth is that, as the apostle Paul writes, 'the creation itself will be liberated from its bondage to decay and brought into the freedom and glory of the children of God' (Romans 8:21). What a mind-boggling choir we'll belong to!

Thank you for your daily provision.
Thank you for your glorious cosmic redemption.

STEPHEN RAND

See what God has done

**Come and see what God has done, his awesome deeds for mankind!…
Praise our God, all peoples, let the sound of his praise be heard; he has
preserved our lives and kept our feet from slipping. For you, God, tested
us; you refined us like silver. You brought us into prison and laid burdens
on our backs. You let people ride over our heads; we went through fire
and water, but you brought us to a place of abundance… Come and hear,
all you who fear God; let me tell you what he has done for me.**

This is a hymn of praise in three sections, each rooted in real-life experience of what God has done. We praise God for who he is, of course. But it
is because of who he is that he acts, and his actions reveal who he is. We
judge everyone's character on the basis of what they say and what they
do – and any gap there is between the two!

God speaks, and action always follows. It was true in the first chapter of
Genesis. It was true for Moses and for David. Their understanding of God was
shaped by seeing him in action: Moses was at the heart of the great deliverance of the exodus; David, the shepherd and king, saw the giant topple.

So the psalmist invites the listener to see what God has done for the
whole human race. He created the universe, he sustains his creation, he
blesses all the peoples of the world with life itself.

Then the writer highlights what God has done for his people. They were
tested, they faced oppression and hardship, but God brought them through
every challenge to a 'place of abundance'. What a beautiful phrase! God is
never careful in his generosity. He doesn't check if things are within budget.
Cups are always overflowing in the land 'flowing with milk and honey'.

Then, says the psalmist, 'let me tell you what he has done for me'. All
these blessings – the provision, the redemption, the abundance – are for
every individual to know and experience. So that means me… and you.

How readily can I answer the question, 'What has God ever done for me?'

STEPHEN RAND

59

A blessing for the world

May God be gracious to us and bless us and make his face shine on us – so that your ways may be known on earth, your salvation among all nations. May the peoples praise you, God; may all the peoples praise you. May the nations be glad and sing for joy, for you rule the peoples with equity and guide the nations of the earth. May the peoples praise you, God; may all the peoples praise you.

Do the opening words of this psalm sound familiar? God instructed Moses to give Aaron a blessing for the people: 'The Lord bless you and keep you; the Lord make his face shine on you and be gracious to you; the Lord turn his face towards you and give you peace' (Numbers 6:24–26). In today's passage, the psalmist echoes those words in his prayer. I find it enormously rewarding to pray using prayers from the Bible, saying them for myself and others. Sometimes we can't find the words to pray, so it's great that God has given us ones we can use.

The writer not only references the ancient beautiful Aaronic blessing, but also links it with God's promise to Abraham: 'I will make you into a great nation, and I will bless you; I will make your name great, and you will be a blessing… all peoples on earth will be blessed through you' (Genesis 12:2–3). He underlines an enormously significant truth – God's blessing is received so that others can be blessed.

That's true for us – we are never meant to just lie back and enjoy God's blessings, but to be energised and blessed again as we share them with others. We are to be channels of God's peace, not blockages. It's true also for the church – are we blessing our community with the strength and enthusiasm with which God has blessed us? And it was true for God's people – they were chosen not because they were special nor simply for their own benefit; they were chosen so that God's ways would be known on earth, his salvation among all nations.

The psalmist's prayer is being answered: 'There before me was a great multitude… from every nation, tribe, people and language, standing before the throne… And they cried out… "Salvation belongs to our God"' (Revelation 7:9–10).

STEPHEN RAND

Songs of praise

Sing to God, sing in praise of his name, extol him who rides on the clouds; rejoice before him – his name is the Lord. A father to the fatherless, a defender of widows, is God in his holy dwelling. God sets the lonely in families, he leads out the prisoners with singing; but the rebellious live in a sun-scorched land.

It's great to worship God with singing. Whether your preferred style is Gregorian chant, cathedral choir or electric guitar and drums, there is something about singing together in full voice that lifts the soul. I still remember the lovely experience as a small boy of going with my father on a Sunday evening and being allowed to sit on the back row of the male voice praise choir while they gave passionate renditions of the old gospel hymns. For many people, one of the hardest things about the recent lockdowns was being cut off from participation in sung worship.

I would love to be able to hear the worship of the time when the psalms were written. No one really knows much about how the psalms were sung; there are one or two biblical hints that it was loud. Sung worship can be a great spiritual experience, as we 'extol him who rides on the clouds'. But to be more than just a good sing, it has to be rooted in reality; then we can worship 'in the Spirit and in truth' (John 4:23). For the psalmist, that reality is about a God who is far more than an ethereal being who lives in the clouds; It is about a God who is focused on the lowly, the bruised and the broken.

There are not many worship songs – old or new – that celebrate God's concern for social justice. The few that do sit uneasily in a culture of worship that most readily celebrates what God has done for individuals in terms of their salvation. Our songs of praise are not an act of escapism; they are directed to the God who is at work in his world.

We worship God by singing with great enthusiasm in church; we worship God by serving our community with equal enthusiasm.

STEPHEN RAND

Suffering for Christ

Lord, the Lord Almighty, may those who hope in you not be disgraced because of me; God of Israel, may those who seek you not be put to shame because of me. For I endure scorn for your sake, and shame covers my face. I am a foreigner to my own family, a stranger to my own mother's children; for zeal for your house consumes me, and the insults of those who insult you fall on me.

I have just once again taken up a role in church leadership. Reading the psalmist's prayer today reminds me of one of the great responsibilities of leadership, which actually applies to all followers of Jesus: all Christians fail at some point; all make mistakes. When we do, it reflects not only on ourselves, but on our church, our fellow Christians – and ultimately on God himself. This is especially true of those in leadership.

Sadly, I've seen it happen all too often. Many years ago, I had an urgent phone call asking whether I could preach on the coming Sunday. The minister's extramarital affair had been uncovered and his resignation accepted, hence the urgency. That Sunday morning the congregation was full of distress and shock.

And people outside the church are quick to latch on. They often have higher standards of behaviour for Christians than they have for themselves, and in one sense they are right to. If we have publicly committed to follow Jesus, then we have publicly committed to living for him and like him.

The second half of today's reading suggests a different context, however. Those 'who endure scorn for your sake' prompts thoughts of the millions of Christians who face persecution because of their faith. One pastor was torn between his faith and his family: if he stood for Christ, he would go to prison and his family would become destitute. He made his decision; he did not want his congregation to be ashamed by his cowardice, and so he was arrested. His son was born just after he went to prison. When he was released after five years, he was a stranger to his own family; his little boy did not know him.

Lord Jesus, be with those who today face violence and insults because of their faith in you.

STEPHEN RAND

Desperation

Hasten, O God, to save me; come quickly, Lord, to help me. May those who want to take my life be put to shame and confusion; may all who desire my ruin be turned back in disgrace. May those who say to me, 'Aha! Aha!' turn back because of their shame. But may all who seek you rejoice and be glad in you; may those who long for your saving help always say, 'The Lord is great!' But as for me, I am poor and needy; come quickly to me, O God. You are my help and my deliverer; Lord, do not delay.

Yesterday we remembered the millions of our sisters and brothers who face persecution. While writing these notes, I've also been interviewed on the radio about the desperate situation in Nigeria, where every day brings news of more Christians murdered by Islamic extremists. Many years ago, my wife visited a church in Nigeria to meet the widows of pastors who had been killed. The door opened to reveal over 400 women had gathered.

It's not unreasonable to imagine that every one of those pastors had prayed, 'Hasten, O God, to save me; come quickly, Lord, to help me.' And for them, it was not to be. Any more than it has been for thousands of others in our day, for hundreds of thousands down through history. We are fairly sure that all but one of Jesus' disciples died a martyr's death. But then all were followers of the one who cried out as he died, 'My God, why have you forsaken me?'

Today you may not be facing death, but you may be poor and needy. Your prayer may well be, 'Come quickly to me, O God.' If that is you, I'm going to ask everyone reading these notes to pray for you. I can't guarantee an immediate miraculous intervention. I can guarantee that God is with you, he will never leave you or forsake you and he will never let you go. He loves you; he loves you for all eternity.

Loving Father, hear our prayer for all who are calling out to you for help and deliverance. May they know your presence and your peace, Amen.

STEPHEN RAND

The letter to the Hebrews

 It is good to have had this opportunity to come to know the letter to the Hebrews more deeply than I had done previously. Some of it had stood out for me before. Jesus' being in the order of Melchizedek seemed obscure, but it was linked in with the theme of hope coming from where we least expect it, which we find in both the Old and New testaments. I had struggled, and still do, with the imagery of temple sacrifice. Yet Hebrews actually supersedes the demands for sacrifice that institutions and we ourselves might make, often for questionable motives. The repetition of short-term, unfulfilling fixes is put aside – Christ has met the need.

Hebrews brings together different cultures and ideas – Greek, Jewish and early Christian – and encourages us to learn, reflect upon and deepen our faith. I love the description of Jesus as 'pioneer and perfecter of our faith' (12:2). It's dynamic, calling us to follow and to explore.

Our churches face great challenges at the moment. Covid-19 has exposed problems in our society and in our churches, throwing us up in the air, and we are beginning to recognise what we treasure and to develop new ways of worship and of being community. Hebrews was written at a time of immense change. What was the church's relationship to the past? What was the significance of the temple ritual, which had once been so sacred? How can the early Christians respond to the threats of persecution?

Hebrews is about working out what is essential, looking back at traditions of courage and sacrifice and then developing language and concepts to express them in Christian terms. The original hearers of these words may have found them painful, exciting and comforting. Jesus is both the fulfiller of tradition and also the forger of a new relationship with God. Hebrews brings together immense concepts, often in the same sentence. I have found this letter quite daunting in the past, but persistence is repaid. The help of some Bible commentaries and companions have been invaluable. I am very glad to be able to share this journey of discovery into Hebrews with you.

HARRY SMART

It's happening now!

Long ago God spoke to our ancestors in many and various ways by the prophets, but in these last days he has spoken to us by a Son, whom he appointed heir of all things, through whom he also created the worlds.

Hebrews begins by linking ancestors, prophets, all creation and all time. The context of the letter is not just a day and year, but the unfolding purposes of God. It's like when pupils write their name and address and then include the Milky Way and the universe. In this letter we are reflecting on that grandeur and are placed in relationship to it.

But lest we get lost in the history of prophets, the events of recent time are brought to the fore. Christ has broken in to time. John's gospel begins with a similar universal vision. Christ is at the beginning of the world but has also dwelt among us.

The letter's recipients had a sense of common ancestry; the prophets are part of their history. We don't know much about these first hearers. They identify with the traditions of the Jews and the temple, as the writer uses these references and knows they will recognise quotes from the Psalms and other texts.

Hebrews often refers to the high priest in the temple. The temple in Jerusalem was destroyed in AD70, so either Hebrews was completed before then or the temple's destruction is the catalyst for the huge change from the earthly high priest to Jesus' sacrifice.

I enjoy history. Learning about other cultures reminds me that our lives now are not the only way of living. History can help us to review where we have come from and find sources of inspiration and warning. Hebrews acknowledges that, but it also reminds us that now is when we are alive: creator and creation meet in this moment. God is revealed in past, present and future.

The church in its different forms carries the message of God's love across the centuries. How do we as church and as individuals respond to change in the church and in our faith?

HARRY SMART

Responsible adults?

Now in subjecting all things to [human beings], God left nothing outside their control. As it is, we do not yet see everything in subjection to them, but we do see Jesus, who for a little while was made lower than the angels, now crowned with glory and honour because of the suffering of death, so that by the grace of God he might taste death for everyone.

Two thousand years on from Hebrews, we see the result of attempting to subject creation to ourselves. At the time the letter was written, the Mediterranean had suffered substantial deforestation. Mountains of broken pottery reveal a problem with waste disposal, which continues to be of interest to archaeologists. Our many environmental catastrophes, from climate change to species loss, show how, since the Industrial Revolution, our connection with nature has been broken. Humans now do have responsibility for our planet, but we seem determined to disregard the integrity of creation.

Believing that we need to be in control has certainly led to great advances. Medical research exists to find a solution to illnesses that otherwise would kill us. I'm not really good with either suffering or pain. I don't see them as goals. In my work as a hospital chaplain, suffering, illness and death are frequently encountered. While the patients I meet often show great resilience, humour and love in the face of life-changing circumstances, suffering is still painful and difficult.

Following a dream of superiority without acknowledging suffering, either our own or that of our environment, causes us to lose our humanity and lose sight of God. Death and suffering need not be failures. We are frail and vulnerable; I see that every day. Christ tastes death for everyone, including nature. Humility and compassion can lead to healing. Christ enters our darkness and brings us the promise of a new way of being. This is about right relationship, not superiority. Christ challenges us to see the world differently.

In our darkness, there is no darkness with you, O Lord.
Help us to rely not so much on our own strength but on your compassion,
creator, lover, redeemer.

HARRY SMART

Handle with care

Every high priest chosen from among mortals is put in charge of things pertaining to God on their behalf, to offer gifts and sacrifices for sins. He is able to deal gently with the ignorant and wayward, since he himself is subject to weakness; and because of this he must sacrifice for his own sins as well as or those of the people. And one does not presume to take this honour, but takes it only when called by God, just as Aaron was.

The high priest is different from the local vicar of popular culture. The language of sacrifice does occur during the Communion service, for example, but it is a sacrifice of 'thanks and praise'. In the service we offer ourselves to be a 'living sacrifice'. We remember Christ's giving of his life for us, sharing himself in bread and wine.

In hospital, at the time of writing, we haven't been able to celebrate Communion in chapel for many months. Whether celebrated on a ward or in a hospital chapel, the presence of God feels close, the kingdom is here. As a priest I am certainly aware of my own weakness – priesthood is not a role that we deserve, and it certainly shouldn't set us above others. In hospital we are stripped of much of the armour that we wear in daily life. I too fall short. We are reminded as Christians to recognise our sin, our falling short, as we prepare to receive Communion, to celebrate God's presence in our world.

As Christians, perhaps we are often perceived as not being aware of our own weaknesses, that we are more ready to exclude than to include. We might seem less willing to celebrate and more likely to criticise. I think that's not an accurate perception: many priests and congregations are welcoming, inspired by the loving and generous God who knows our weaknesses and still calls us to know him.

As part of the priesthood of all believers, how can I deal more gently and kindly with others, including myself?

HARRY SMART

Finding sustenance

You need milk, not solid food... Solid food is for the mature, for those whose faculties have been trained by practice to distinguish good from evil. Therefore let us go on towards perfection, leaving behind the basic teaching about Christ, and not laying again the foundation.

I sometimes encounter patients who tell me that they went to Sunday school, so now they know enough about faith and God. Often Sunday school was long ago. Often it's said with a sense of resentment or self-justification. Perhaps it's seeing the dog collar that does it!

The author of Hebrews is trying to encourage his hearers. He doesn't want to dishearten them, but he wants to lead them forwards from the basics to more in-depth faith. Childlike faith can be very moving. The trust that I have witnessed in some, despite their circumstances, is truly inspiring. It isn't naive, but it is full of love, generosity and a sense of God's presence. It isn't childish, though it might be cheeky!

This is quite different, however, from faith that has not developed beyond infancy. There can be a lack of preparation for the trials of adulthood and its questions and insights. Faith that is over-protected, either by the individual or by their church, is close to being confined in aspic. It can be rejected or seem to be sustained on life support, doing little to help grow and nourish when life gets hard.

Telling the difference between good and evil isn't easy, though often people will say they can do it. Jesus is cautious, advising his disciples not to get rid of the weeds in the field lest they pull up the crops as well. What may be good for some things harms others, as the corncockle that grows in our garden has taught me – it's great for bees but poisonous for chickens.

As we grow in faith, we tend to become less concerned about some of the boundaries and sharp definitions that troubled us before. But that doesn't mean we have to accept everything.

What has helped you grow in your faith?

HARRY SMART

Keep going!

Even though we speak in this way, beloved, we are confident of better things in your case, things that belong to salvation. For God is not unjust; he will not overlook your work and the love that you showed for his sake in serving the saints, as you still do.

If you have a lot to learn it helps to have a good teacher. There is an urgency to this letter that might not seem clear at first, with its complex and perhaps obscure high priest imagery. The writer wants his hearers to listen, grow and develop. He has encouraged them to move beyond their basic understanding of faith and also to keep true to God. They have already been through suffering – alluded to in Hebrews 10:34. This inclines me to feel that the temple has been destroyed. There is a lot to learn quickly, and it may be that realising their new identity outside of the community that looks towards the temple is part of that.

The writer of Hebrews encourages and warns his hearers. He praises them for doing well, but one or two comments suggest that he is frustrated by some. Perhaps they are afraid; perhaps they feel they are moving too far from their original identity.

During the first lockdown, when all churches were closed, our parish, like others, began new ways of doing things. We have worshipped online with the Methodists. We were anxious about returning to physical worship, but still people came. How do we continue as church in our town? The same story could be told around the world. Financial restrictions will demand more from lay people than even before.

The writer of Hebrews praises the love that the church has shown. Are the saints that are referred to here church leaders, perhaps those who have been persecuted? It is work and love that commends the community to God. And surely those need to be at the heart of any congregation.

Think of the congregation of which you are a part. What examples of work, love and service do you see? How can you celebrate these?

HARRY SMART

Faith, hope and love

There is, on the one hand, the abrogation of an earlier commandment because it was weak and ineffectual (for the law made nothing perfect); there is, on the other hand, the introduction of a better hope, through which we approach God.

Hebrews' exploration of Jesus' priesthood in the order of Melchizedek seems quite obscure. It's a story that is not well-known to most, I suspect. The point is being made that Jesus, who was neither a Levite nor a high priest in his earthly life, follows more closely the pattern of the king who is also a priest, who blessed and was therefore superior to Abraham. The Dead Sea Scrolls portray Melchizedek as returning to bring salvation and judgement at the end of the world. Melchizedek may have been more significant in some Jewish thought than we are aware.

The apostle Paul places hope alongside faith and love as key in our catching a glimpse of God. But hope in the ancient world was quite ambiguous. When Pandora opens the box, releasing the tribulations of life on to the world, hope is also included in the box. She releases it, perhaps to counteract everything else, but perhaps because it can, if unfounded, simply increase suffering. Hope was either an affliction or a source of strength.

For Hebrews, hope is grounded in God's action revealed through history and time. Past events have spoken of God's action, even in dark times; for example, Jeremiah in the besieged Jerusalem. The writer of Hebrews will have held on to memories of past events and looked to the future of the coming of Christ.

Sometimes patients speak to me of giving up hope, having lost their way. I may ask what has kept them going in difficult times, what brings them a sense of purpose or when have they had a sense of God in the past. Hope isn't the same as pretending that pain isn't real. That would be cruel. Hope speaks of the core of where meaning and purpose are. There we can begin to approach God.

As Christians what do we hope for?

HARRY SMART

A foretaste

They offer worship in a sanctuary that is a sketch and shadow of the heavenly one; for Moses, when he was about to erect the tent, was warned, 'See that you make everything according to the pattern that was shown you on the mountain.' But Jesus has now obtained a more excellent ministry, and to that degree he is the mediator of a better covenant.

Hebrews is written in a period of great change. The temple may have been destroyed, emphasising the need for changes in practice and understanding. Judaism was already changing to a more rabbinical expression rather than temple-based one. The early Christians were also having to reflect on their identity. Greek thought predominated across the Roman empire and this brought new ideas to Judaism and to Christianity.

Philo of Alexandria was a Jewish theologian writing during the period of Jesus' life. Living away from the temple and Jerusalem, he developed a more metaphorical understanding of some of the biblical narratives and teaching. He was heavily influenced by the Greek philosopher Plato, who saw this world as a shadow of reality. Plato's image of people in a cave seeing only the shadows of life playing on the walls and not turning around to see their origin is famous.

The earthly temple is a foretaste of the heavenly one, and Christ is the real high priest. Jesus establishes a new covenant, which goes beyond that revealed by Moses.

Christianity was being formed in a time of change, influenced by contemporary ideas, and it has continued to be so. Through reflection on historical and political events, from plagues to concentration camps and climate change, Christianity has rediscovered and re-expressed truths, helping us to more greatly appreciate God.

My faith has developed over the years too. Many of the emphases are still there. Meditation has been a clear thread, and the desire to put faith into practice. But some concerns have shifted, some of my attitudes have become gentler.

Has your faith changed over the years? What have been the main threads that run through it for you?

HARRY SMART

Looking back, looking forward

'They shall not teach one another or say to each other, "Know the Lord", for they shall all know me, from the least of them to the greatest. For I will be merciful towards their iniquities, and I will remember their sins no more.' In speaking of 'a new covenant', he has made the first one obsolete. And what is obsolete and growing old will soon disappear.

'Where there is no vision, the people perish' is a well-known quote from Proverbs 29:18 (KJV). It harks back to the situation Moses faced when the Israelites were rebelling from his direction. Most of the verses that Hebrews is using here quote Jeremiah 31:31–34. Jeremiah was almost a second Moses for the post-exilic community. Faced by invading armies, Jeremiah speaks of forgiveness and hope, of a new relationship with God.

Throughout the Old Testament, God promises the Jewish people a new covenant, from the very creation of Adam, through flood, childlessness, kingdom and exile. Jeremiah holds out the hope that Jerusalem will be enlarged. In the face of the Babylonians, he buys land, ordering the deeds to be carefully preserved for the future. At some time, the exiles will return.

Hebrews has extended that promise. The covenant isn't only for the geographical Jerusalem, threatened or destroyed as it had been. Jesus had warned that the temple would be destroyed, but that he would rise again. He wept for the city that killed the prophets. Hebrews speaks of new hope, not for one city but in Christ.

As a chaplain, I frequently listen to people telling me stories. Some are overwhelmed by illness, by the threat of change or of pain. But more often they tell of family and friends, beginning to rediscover themselves as they speak. There is something sacred about the encounter. Sometimes I will pray with them, and often I will simply give a blessing. It's a reaffirmation that God is with them, a part of their healing process.

In what way can Christians be people of hope?

HARRY SMART

Can we accept it?

When he said above, 'You have neither desired nor taken pleasure in sacrifices and offerings and burnt-offerings and sin-offerings' (these are offered according to the law), then he added, 'See, I have come to do your will'… And it is by God's will that we have been sanctified through the offering of the body of Jesus Christ once for all.

The 21st century may seem a long way from the sacrifice of sheep and goats, though the over-consumption of meat is a major cause of ecological damage. Working with stressed nurses and, in my chaplaincy work, with patients with mental health problems, I believe we have tended to sacrifice ourselves and others too. For many people, work demands the sacrifice of health and contentment.

Having witnessed the bravery of health-care staff during the Covid crisis, I know that for some that courage has meant a sacrifice of secure health. Supermarket staff have risked their own safety in the face of people's anger at the lack of supplies. But even before Covid, many made themselves ill at work. At first, this may not seem like the sacrifices offered in the temple, but often it is justified by the need to maintain the economy or keep the machine running. We may take such sacrifices for granted. I am aware of injustice in trade and of the damage done by food miles or using my car rather than public transport. Yet I often sacrifice these for my convenience.

The prophets were clear about sacrifices too. Hosea has God saying, 'I desire steadfast love and not sacrifice, the knowledge of God rather than burnt-offerings' (Hosea 6:6). Micah, too, questions such sacrifice: 'What does the Lord require of you but to do justice, and to love kindness, and to walk humbly with your God?' (Micah 6:8).

If we can accept that Christ gave his life for us, can we begin to move away from the tendency to sacrifice ourselves and God's creation?

HARRY SMART

Just ahead

Therefore, since we are surrounded by so great a cloud of witnesses, let us lay aside every weight and the sin that clings so closely, and let us run with perseverance the race that is set before us, looking to Jesus the pioneer and perfecter of our faith.

There are times in our worship and our lives when we recollect those who inspire us or about whom we are concerned. Our intercessions for those who are ill bring us closer to those who suffer. Memorial celebrations of friends and loved ones do so too, bringing close those who have inspired us and who have been dear. I remember taking a Christian Aid service in a Norman church, where the thoughts and experiences of others were brought vividly to life – a connection had been formed between apparently different worlds.

Hebrews here is thinking of those who have suffered within the Jewish community. The witnesses had suffered persecution for their faith. Hebrews sees those who have suffered in the past as encouraging us, urging us on.

Suffering can isolate us. We may seem the only ones enduring the pain. Sadly, often patients are separated from relatives and friends, especially now. Hebrews uses the image of the Greek athlete stripping off and running before thousands of spectators. What could be an isolating experience becomes one where the athlete is encouraged by others. These are those who have died but also the living.

I wasn't good at running, not since cross-country runs in the mud. But my dad enjoyed watching horse racing, so I remember Lester Piggott, the flat-racing jockey. He developed his own style, high in the stirrups, parallel to the horse, fast and aerodynamic. He was a pioneer and perfecter. Jockeys have emulated him since.

Jesus is the pioneer and perfecter of our faith – leading us forward, through pain, but promising joy.

Are you running, walking, taking a breather? Who is alongside you?
Can you relieve yourself of some of the things that weigh you down
and catch a glimpse of Jesus, just ahead?

HARRY SMART

Outside the city wall

Jesus also suffered outside the city gate in order to sanctify the people by his own blood. Let us then go to him outside the camp and bear the abuse he endured. For here we have no lasting city, but we are looking for the city that is to come.

The sacrifices made by the high priest would have been in the temple in Jerusalem. Jesus, because he was executed as a criminal, died on the cross outside the city limits. This becomes symbolic of the movement away from Judaism and the temple system, which Hebrews is addressing.

Dietrich Bonhoeffer, in his *Letters and Papers from Prison*, written during captivity by the SS, wrote in a poem of how Jesus stands with us in our suffering and how we stand alongside him in his. Bonhoeffer was afraid, though described by others as being calm. But he knew that, by taking the stance he did against Hitler from the first, he might pay the ultimate price. Jesus' sacrifice for us doesn't excuse us from acting for justice or being alongside those people and environments where abuse is taking place.

Jesus' life and teaching and the manner of his death put him alongside those suffering injustice. The Christians of the later first century AD weren't undergoing great persecution, but Hebrews does speak of torture and imprisonment. We aren't called to martyr ourselves deliberately. Hebrews warns us from sacrificing ourselves – there is one sacrifice. But there is a restlessness, a discontent with the accepted mainstream that brings a sense of homelessness. The earthly city may rely on victims and on exclusion. The new Jerusalem has gates that are open, the river of healing flows through it.

Bonhoeffer resisted the compromises that parts of the church made with Hitler. He began to create underground Christian communities that were to continue a sense of identity and resistance under pressure. Often standing alongside Jesus outside the city will bring challenges and criticism. Sometimes it will cost our lives.

Have there been times when you have felt 'outside of the city'.
Where has Christ been for you then?

HARRY SMART

Cure of souls

Obey your leaders and submit to them, for they are keeping watch over your souls and will give an account. Let them do this with joy and not with sighing – for that would be harmful to you. Pray for us; we are sure that we have a clear conscience, desiring to act honourably in all things.

The leaders in this case are presumably leaders of the church – they specifically have the responsibility for souls. At their licensing, Church of England clergy are given the 'cure of souls' by their bishop 'which is both yours and mine'. It's a shared responsibility between bishop and clergy for those in the parish. While we may protest that no one has responsibility for our souls but ourselves, we do accept that we share responsibility for one another. A manager has responsibility for their colleagues – a ward or team is very affected by its management.

We may suspect our leaders of all sorts of failures or machinations. We may tend to assume that they have little or no idea of how things really are where we are. Perhaps we can be a little more generous towards our leaders. The cure of souls is the responsibility of all of us, and 2,000 years on we tend to be more egalitarian and democratic. But responsibility for others brings enough challenges; publicly representing the church and in some way the kingdom of God is almost impossible.

Managing small chaplaincy teams over many years has been enough to show me how difficult the multiplicity of roles in leadership can be. Hebrews asks his hearers to pray for him. He has a clear conscience – is he quite sure? As a teacher of faith, he bears huge responsibility. Could he have imagined his words would be read today?

Sometimes our leaders need encouragement and generosity, sometimes they need to be held to account. But they are no less human than we ourselves.

We have responsibility, too. How do we help our leaders to be good at what they do?

HARRY SMART

Turn but a stone

Let mutual love continue. Do not neglect to show hospitality to strangers, for by doing that some have entertained angels without knowing it. Remember those who are in prison, as though you were in prison with them.

Some have entertained angels without knowing it, writes Hebrews. Following the grand scale of Hebrews' vision, this is a verse that I love. Hospitality was highly rated in the Mediterranean world. Life was unpredictable, and travellers were to be treated well. Welcoming an angel is risky. From Sarah and Abraham, who hurry to entertain and feed the three visiting angels and are told that they will have a son, to Lot, who offers hospitality to two angels in the risky environment of Sodom, to Mary's assent to God's plan announced by the angel Gabriel, angels have heralded life-changing news. Jacob wrestled with an angel and was blessed.

When we see others as angels, life begins to change. I may begin to think that I have heard a patient's story often before, then I notice a detail that strikes me so freshly or something they say seems like a pin prick. Spiritual directors have been able to put their finger gently and kindly on issues I've needed to address. Angels can be loud and clear or encouraging and loving.

In mental health chaplaincy, I enjoyed the frankness with which patients might speak about their concerns and experiences. They weren't intended to impress, but to share difficult circumstances, which needed to be met with equal honesty (provided you are professional). I think of the homeless people I encountered and am inspired by the care they showed each other. Angels don't always make easy dinner companions, but they are certainly memorable.

Entertaining angels is followed by praying for prisoners. Are these Christians? Hebrews doesn't say so, but it would follow Hebrew's advice to be aware and attentive to guests that we should be reminded to pray for and visit those who are among the most forgotten and despised.

Have you ever entertained an angel? What was their message?
Have you been an angel?

HARRY SMART

Peace and completeness

Now may the God of peace , who brought back from the dead our Lord Jesus , the great shepherd of the sheep, by the blood of the eternal covenant, make you complete in everything good so that you may do his will.

We have seen how good Hebrews is at bringing together many themes in very few verses. In this benediction, he unites the main threads of the entire epistle. With all its imagery of the temple, high priest and sacrifice it is good to be reminded that God's blessing is peace. Rest has been emphasised as a quality of being with God. Peace is an attribute too – God is the fulfilling of our desire and searching, as this world is only a partial reflection of the fulness of God. Our restlessness, our mere fleeting glimpses of peace, are borne from our hope for completion.

Like a Middle Eastern shepherd, whose sheep follow him, Jesus leads us forward in a role reminiscent of Moses. But Jesus' covenant is complete, says Hebrews, not needing to be reasserted year upon year. We too are set free from the need to justify ourselves year upon year. We can begin to be motivated not by a need to prove ourselves, but by the peace of God.

There are times when I have the sense of that peace. Practising mindfulness with others, I begin to get beyond my own thoughts to a calm beyond me, but not alien to me. Sitting quietly, aware of our breathing, something speaks to me of God breathing in me and all creation. Then, as I ring the bell to bring the session to an end, the care staff I have been meditating with prepare to return to their patients and responsibilities.

I also find peace during my walks in the woodland, the relationship with God and connection to nature is close for me. Christ's resurrection is there, raising me too. I don't always feel complete, but sometimes I am aware that I am held by God.

When have you felt closest to the peace of God?

HARRY SMART

Job

 The book of Job grapples with one of the most fundamental questions of human existence – why do innocent people suffer? We can understand that those who do wrong will suffer, for there is a kind of natural justice in that. The problem comes when those who have done nothing wrong find themselves afflicted. That seems quite unfair.

In early 2020 these issues became real for me. After four years of gruelling treatment for breast cancer, my wife was diagnosed as terminally ill with no more treatment options available. The cancer had spread to her spine, and quickly her condition deteriorated. We tried to look after Evelyn at home, but her needs were too great. Eventually she went into a local care home. This was the time of lockdown, because of coronavirus. I decided to go with her as a temporary resident because otherwise I would not be able to see her.

We had six good weeks together, but she was becoming weaker. Then we both contracted the virus, and while surprisingly Evelyn soon got over it, I was admitted to hospital and intensive care. After I recovered, I could no longer join her in the care home, so we were separated until a few days before she died when we could visit her.

Studying the book of Job has been therapeutic. Not that I have been railing against God as Job did, but because it has helped me to appreciate again the mystery that surrounds human suffering. There are no simple formulas to explain why we suffer. At the end of the day, it is a matter of trust.

This is a long book, and the arguments are often complicated and involved, but in between the rhetoric are nuggets of spiritual gold, profound insights into the nature of the human condition and the ways of God. It is not an easy book to read, but it has an abiding relevance, especially when we find ourselves suffering unjustly or unnecessarily and we wonder why.

Job is remembered for his example of patience and perseverance (James 5:10–11). These are qualities we each need to develop as we seek to be disciples in a world where suffering abounds and will inevitably one day come knocking on our door.

TONY HORSFALL

Living the good life

In the land of Uz there lived a man whose name was Job. This man was blameless and upright; he feared God and shunned evil. He had seven sons and three daughters, and he owned seven thousand sheep, three thousand camels, five hundred yoke of oxen and five hundred donkeys, and had a large number of servants. He was the greatest man among all the people of the East.

We are introduced to Job and can immediately see that he is a good man. His deep faith was expressed in the way he lived. He feared God, which means he had a deep reverence for God and took his faith seriously. He sought to live his life according to the instructions of God and to do what was right. This he did meticulously.

Job was also a family man, having been blessed with a wife and children. They were mostly grown up at this point, and they enjoy a good party (1:4, 13). Sometimes they would celebrate to excess, and to make sure that they were still right with God, Job would offer sacrifices on their behalf, such was his scrupulosity. What parent hasn't had similar worries about their children?

Job was also a great man, successful in everything he did, and well-known and respected in his community. His wealth is shown in the size of his flocks. No doubt he also owned houses and lands.

Here is a picture of a man contentedly living the good life. He has obeyed God, and God has blessed him abundantly. He is living the dream, and apart from the occasional anxious thought about his children, his world is at peace. At this moment he has no inkling how his world will soon be turned upside down. He has found the formula for successful and happy living, and he thinks that nothing can disturb his contentment.

Like Job, most of us are taken aback when suffering breaks into our lives. One moment we are happy and content, the next our lives are in pieces. This is why our faith must be well-grounded, and we must have a truly biblical understanding of suffering.

Lord, plant my feet on solid ground so that when the storms blow,
I am not blown over.

TONY HORSFALL

A peep behind the scenes

Then the Lord said to Satan, 'Have you considered my servant Job? There is no one on earth like him; he is blameless and upright, a man who fears God and shuns evil.' 'Does Job fear God for nothing?' Satan replied. 'Have you not put a hedge around him and his household and everything he has? You have blessed the work of his hands, so that his flocks and herds are spread throughout the land. But now stretch out your hand and strike everything he has, and he will surely curse you to your face.'

We may be surprised to see God and Satan in conversation, but it is not so much a friendly chat as a throwing down of the gauntlet to the enemy of souls. Satan has been roaming the earth, up to his usual mischief of enticing people to sin (v. 7). God, as a kind of challenge, draws Satan's attention to Job, a man in whom the Lord has great delight because of his strong faith and upright life.

Satan does not believe that human beings can love God for God's own sake. Rather, he suggests, people like Job believe only for what they can get from God. It is blessing they want, not him. Material prosperity is what they are really after, Satan says, and if that is removed, they will soon stop believing in God. The challenge is accepted and given certain limitations; Satan is allowed to remove the hedge of protection from around Job and his family.

This, then, is the background to the sufferings of Job, of which both he and his friends are totally unaware. Unwittingly, Job finds himself caught up in the cosmic strife between heaven and hell, and his life is the battleground. Through his circumstances, it will be seen if a human being can truly love God for God's own sake. Much is at stake.

What about us? Why do we believe in God? What is our real motivation? The tests of life reveal what is really in our hearts, and whether we love God for who he is or for what he gives. Suffering shows what we are made of and what we really believe.

Lord, help me to love you sincerely, and not for any hoped-for benefits.

TONY HORSFALL

The ultimate in loss

While he was still speaking, yet another messenger came and said, 'Your sons and daughters were feasting and drinking wine at the eldest brother's house, when suddenly a mighty wind swept in from the desert and struck the four corners of the house. It collapsed on them and they are dead, and I am the only one who has escaped to tell you!' At this, Job got up and tore his robe and shaved his head. Then he fell to the ground in worship and said: 'Naked I came from my mother's womb, and naked I will depart. The Lord gave and the Lord has taken away; may the name of the Lord be praised.' In all this, Job did not sin by charging God with wrongdoing.

It is one thing to lose your possessions, but another to lose your children. Things can be replaced, but people can't. No parent expects to see their children die before them. We can only imagine the horror that Job and his wife must have felt as they received the tragic news that their children had been wiped out in a freak accident. How would you or I cope in the face of such dreadful loss? How would we respond? What impact would it have on our faith?

A natural response is to blame God for such an occurrence: 'If God loves me why did he allow this to happen?' This is a common complaint. In grief, we look for someone to blame, and the Almighty is an obvious target. Faith that is not well grounded can easily cave in when faced with tragedy.

Job, however, is made of sterner stuff. Yes, he grieves, but he also chooses to worship. Rather than turning away from God in his moment of need, he turns towards God. The sacrifice of praise forms on his lips, and he offers himself and his suffering to the God he serves. Satan is proved wrong. Here is a man who does fear God even when the chips are down. God's delight in his servant is vindicated. It is possible for a person to love God without ulterior motive.

Lord, may we find grace to trust you in our suffering and to worship you despite painful circumstances.

TONY HORSFALL

Faith among the ashes

So Satan went out from the presence of the Lord and afflicted Job with painful sores from the soles of his feet to the crown of his head. Then Job took a piece of broken pottery and scraped himself with it as he sat among the ashes. His wife said to him, 'Are you still maintaining your integrity? Curse God and die!' He replied, 'You are talking like a foolish woman. Shall we accept good from God, and not trouble?' In all this, Job did not sin in what he said.

Having so far failed to undermine Job's faith, Satan is granted permission to test him even further by afflicting him physically with painful sores. From what we read elsewhere in the book this was a disease that developed rapidly and spread throughout his body, rendering him helpless and in despair. Again, Satan's reasoning is that human beings are basically self-centred and concerned only for themselves. If Job himself is touched personally by misfortune, he will surely capitulate.

Again, Satan has greatly underestimated Job's strength of character and the reality of his faith. Despite his affliction he refuses to curse God or to sin by charging God with evil. He shows remarkable courage and resilience in the face of great provocation. Even his wife's discouraging call to give it all up will not persuade him to yield.

Notice here the word 'integrity'. This is very important in understanding Job. His integrity refers to his commitment to follow God no matter what happens. He is no fair-weather believer. It matters deeply to him that he maintains his faith and does not turn against God. He does not wish to sin, even when under such pressure. This is why he will so strongly resist the suggestion from his friends that his suffering is actually the result of his sin. His integrity is at stake.

Perhaps you worry about your own faith. Remember that God is faithful, and he will not allow you to be tempted beyond what you can bear (1 Corinthians 10:13). Very few of us will be called to suffer like Job. What matters is that we are faithful to God in the midst of our own trials.

Lord, may I be found faithful, even in the day of trial.

TONY HORSFALL

What friends are for

When Job's three friends, Eliphaz the Temanite, Bildad the Shuhite and Zophar the Naamathite, heard about all the troubles that had come upon him, they set out from their homes and met together by agreement to go and sympathise with him and comfort him. When they saw him from a distance, they could hardly recognise him; they began to weep aloud, and they tore their robes and sprinkled dust on their heads. Then they sat on the ground with him for seven days and seven nights. No one said a word to him, because they saw how great his suffering was.

Friends are a great resource in times of need. In his crisis, Job finds he is not alone. Three friends come to see him – Eliphaz, Bildad and Zophar. They appear to be older men, respected in the community for their wisdom and spiritual authority. Although later Job will call them 'worthless physicians' (13:4) and 'miserable comforters' (16:2), they make a promising start.

They arrive with an agreed purpose, to sympathise with Job and to comfort him. These are noble aims and what bereaved people and those who are unwell need most of all. If they had stayed with this simple objective, they may not have fallen out with their friend!

They were also deeply touched by Job's condition, and his plight causes them to weep and feel his grief. This kind of emotional connection is exemplary and illustrates the New Testament exhortation to weep with those who weep (Romans 12:15). We do not have to be stiff and formal when we seek to comfort others, we can feel what they feel and identify with their pain.

Perhaps the greatest gift they brought to Job, however, was the gift of their silence. They simply sat with him for seven days and nights without speaking. Sometimes words are unnecessary. Indeed, often they can be a hindrance. They avoided the trap of speaking for the sake of saying something and of offering advice or pious platitudes.

What would you want from your friends if you were in need? What do you learn today about how to approach others in their pain?

Lord, thank you for my friends. May I be a wise and sensitive helper of others.

TONY HORSFALL

Sowing and reaping

'If someone ventures a word with you, will you be impatient? But who can keep from speaking?… But now trouble comes to you, and you are discouraged; it strikes you, and you are dismayed… Consider now: who, being innocent, has ever perished? Where were the upright destroyed? As I have observed, those who plough evil and those who sow trouble reap it. At the breath of God they perish; at the blast of his anger they are no more.'

Eliphaz appears the most senior of the friends and is the first to respond after Job breaks the silence (Job 3). His understanding of Job's suffering is that he has brought it upon himself. His theology of suffering is that we reap what we sow. If we sin, we will suffer. If we disobey God, there will be consequences. Suffering is therefore God's way of disciplining us: 'Blessed is the one whom God corrects; so do not despise the discipline of the Almighty' (5:17).

This understanding is common throughout the Bible, and there is truth in it. Under the Mosaic covenant obedience brings blessing and disobedience a curse (Deuteronomy 28). Whenever Israel obeyed the Lord, they were blessed; whenever they rebelled, they suffered painfully. This is the principle that Eliphaz seeks to apply to Job's situation without knowing the full story. Job is suffering; he must have sinned.

When things go wrong in our lives, it is worth asking, 'Have I brought this trouble upon myself? Is God disciplining me, waking me up to my foolish behaviour so I can turn away from it?' If this is the case, we will know already what we have done wrong. If we are wise, we will turn away from any wrong behaviour.

But this is not the reason for Job's suffering. To apply this principle to his situation is damaging and hurtful. He has done nothing to warrant such enormous pain. How important it is to be sensitive to people and not jump to conclusions. Suffering is seldom a direct consequence of sin. There is a mystery behind suffering, and we should be careful not to rigidly apply principles that may be true in some circumstances but not all.

Lord, help me not to be rigid in my assessment of others.

TONY HORSFALL

My integrity is at stake

'Teach me, and I will be quiet; show me where I have been wrong. How painful are honest words! But what do your arguments prove? Do you mean to correct what I say, and treat my desperate words as wind?... But now be so kind as to look at me. Would I lie to your face? Relent, do not be unjust; reconsider, for my integrity is at stake. Is there any wickedness on my lips? Can my mouth not discern malice?'

The discussion between Job and his friends quickly escalates into a fiery debate. Although they have come to help him, Job does not welcome the suggestion that his suffering is the result of sin. He is adamant he has done nothing wrong and does not deserve to be suffering at all.

Honesty is important in friendship, and a wise person must be willing to be corrected by those who have their best interests at heart. Job invites his friends to take a good look at him, not only to see the state he is in but also to recognise he is speaking the truth. His face tells its own story.

Job's integrity is based around the fact that he has not knowingly sinned against God. He is not claiming sinless perfection, only that, as far as he knows, he has not broken any commandments or neglected any ritual requirements. In that sense he is blameless and righteous. His friends should know this since they have seen his lifestyle and character. He has done nothing to warrant the degree of suffering that has come upon him. The principle that the righteous prosper and the wicked suffer cannot therefore be valid in his case.

Job will continue to protest his innocence. He will complain that God is unfair and demand a hearing with him where he can put his case (7:11–16, 10:1–2). The friends for their part will remain adamant that he has sinned, sticking fast to their doctrine even though the facts contradict it.

As friends we have the right to speak openly with each other, but we must always beware of going too far or of insensitively misapplying the truth we promote.

Lord, help me to speak the truth, but always in love.

TONY HORSFALL

Why not simply repent?

Then Bildad the Shuhite replied: 'How long will you say such things? Your words are a blustering wind. Does God pervert justice? Does the Almighty pervert what is right? When your children sinned against him, he gave them over to the penalty of their sin. But if you will seek God earnestly and plead with the Almighty, if you are pure and upright, even now he will rouse himself on your behalf and restore you to your prosperous state.'

Joan declared, 'I always say what I think'. Her friend replied, 'Yes, but do you always think what you say?' Bildad is the kind of person who thinks aloud and doesn't consider the implications of his words. How wounding it must have been for Job to hear in such a blunt way that his children had perished because of their sin. No wonder he was mad with his friends. They add to his misery by their callous disregard for his feelings.

Bildad wants to defend the reputation of God. Job accuses God of being unjust, but that cannot be right. God is a God of justice, and he can never be unfair. The fault must lie with Job, Bildad reasons, even if he is unaware of his sin. If only Job would repent and earnestly seek forgiveness, he would discover that God is also merciful and will pardon him and restore his fortunes.

Here is the deadlock between Job and his friends, and the arguments go back and forth throughout the middle section of the book. It is a classic case of two parties not really listening to what the other is saying. They have taken up entrenched positions, which they fiercely defend. Neither has the full understanding of what is happening or why Job is suffering, so how can they find the truth? They are all speaking out of ignorance.

This is a trap that religious people easily fall into. Because we hold truth very dearly (at least our perceptions of truth), we feel we must defend it with our lives. Conflict ensues because we do not have the humility to listen to others or to be open to other possible opinions.

Lord, help me know when to close my mouth and when to open my heart.

TONY HORSFALL

A glimpse of Jesus?

'Oh, that my words were recorded, that they were written on a scroll, that they were inscribed with an iron tool on lead, or engraved in rock forever! I know that my redeemer lives, and that in the end he will stand on the earth. And after my skin has been destroyed, yet in my flesh I will see God; I myself will see him with my own eyes – I, and not another. How my heart yearns within me!'

Here we have some of the most well-known words in the whole book, made famous by their inclusion in Handel's *Messiah*. The great composer had no doubt that Job was speaking here of the coming Messiah, even if many contemporary Bible scholars reject the idea.

It may be that this is not a direct prophecy about the Messiah, but it is certainly, in my view, a wistful longing for such a person. This yearning occurs at regular intervals throughout the speeches made by Job. He longs for someone to arbitrate or mediate between himself and God (9:33). He speaks about having a 'witness in heaven', an advocate and an intercessor to plead his case with the Almighty (16:19–21). And here he speaks about a redeemer (v. 25). In his pain, Job is acutely aware of his need for help from outside himself. He longs for a Saviour.

The idea of a redeemer (Hebrew *goel*) is found in Leviticus 25, and describes a close relative who comes to the aid of a distressed family member. Boaz acts like this as kinsman-redeemer for Ruth and Naomi, buying back their land and taking responsibility for them both (Ruth 4:1–10). The picture, then, is of someone who comes to our aid and rescues us in a time of peril, at considerable personal cost.

All of us have felt this longing for a helper when we have been overwhelmed by life. It is a natural human response, a God-given instinct because it points us away from ourselves and towards him. This is one of the great gifts of suffering. It can awaken in us our need for God. Whether Job knew it or not, his longing was clearly fulfilled in the coming of Jesus Christ, the great Redeemer.

Lord, in you I place my trust.

TONY HORSFALL

A wave of grief

Job continued his discourse: 'How I long for the months gone by, for the days when God watched over me, when his lamp shone on my head and by his light I walked through darkness! Oh, for the days when I was in my prime, when God's intimate friendship blessed my house, when the Almighty was still with me and my children were around me, when my path was drenched with cream and the rock poured out for me streams of olive oil.'

So far, Job has appeared quite dispassionate about his suffering. He has become embattled with his friends and has had no time to grieve. Now his emotions catch up with him, and he remembers better days. He is reminded of all he has lost.

As I write, I find myself identifying with Job. When my wife passed away in the middle of 2020, after her long battle with cancer, I experienced at first a feeling of relief that she was no longer suffering. For a while I was protected emotionally by a sense of unreality, as if it had not really happened. Then the bubble burst and I realised the enormity of my loss. It dawned on me that life would never be the same again. At that point the past seemed a more attractive option than either the present or the future. I too longed 'for the months gone by'.

Grief is the price we pay for loving and it is a valid and normal emotional response, not to be denied or suppressed. Grief accompanies any loss, not just a bereavement, and it takes time for it to work itself through. Sometimes we may feel that we will never heal, that the pain will always be with us. I find it comes to me in waves. Just as I think I am through the worst, another wave of longing and yearning for the past sweeps over me, triggered by the tiniest thing.

This brief glimpse of Job's humanity is a reminder to us that we need not hide our grief. The compassionate Father waits to comfort us, and so do our relatives and friends. Whatever your grief, there is no need to suffer in silence or alone.

Father of mercy, heal my hurting heart.

TONY HORSFALL

Remember who God is

'Now no one can look at the sun, bright as it is in the skies after the wind has swept them clean. Out of the north he comes in golden splendour; God comes in awesome majesty. The Almighty is beyond reach and exalted in power; in his justice and great righteousness he does not oppress. Therefore, people revere him, for does he not have regard for all the wise in heart?'

Elihu is young but confident his words are from God. Having listened to the debate between Job and his friends, he reminds them (chapters 32—37) of God's greatness and that he is just in all his ways. He also believes that suffering is caused by sin and that God disciplines us through affliction, but his focus is more on the fact that God is beyond our understanding and we cannot fathom his ways.

This is a new dimension to the argument and one with validity. In our scientific age, we believe that there is a rational explanation for everything and that we can understand why things happen. Some things, however, such as suffering, remain beyond our reach. In this life, we may not be able to give a reason for everything. We are called to trust, not to understand.

To bolster his argument, Elihu describes his experience of meeting God in a storm: 'God's voice thunders in marvellous ways; he does great things beyond our understanding' (37:5). If you have ever been caught in a violent storm, you will know how tiny one feels before the majesty of God. When Job is protesting his innocence and demanding an audience with God, he is forgetting that he is addressing the Almighty. If he were really wise, he would humbly keep silent and acknowledge his sin.

How easy it is to reduce God to our level and make him accountable to our human understanding, but what folly that is. Sometimes we must bow silently before his superior wisdom and awesome power and trust that he knows what he is doing. 'Oh, the depth of the riches of the wisdom and knowledge of God! How unsearchable his judgements, and his paths beyond tracing out' (Romans 11:33).

Lord, help me humbly acknowledge your majesty
and gladly accept my limitations.

TONY HORSFALL

Found wanting

Then the Lord spoke to Job out of the storm. He said: 'Who is this that obscures my plans with words without knowledge? Brace yourself like a man; I will question you, and you shall answer me. Where were you when I laid the earth's foundation? Tell me, if you understand. Who marked off its dimensions? Surely you know! Who stretched a measuring line across it?'

It is every student's worst nightmare – an exam paper in which you don't know the answer to a single question! Just when you thought you were pretty clever, you realise you are actually quite foolish.

That must have been Job's response to the interrogation he receives from God, the creator of the universe. His appalling ignorance is revealed, and he is shown up for his lack of knowledge. Having longed for a meeting with God, when it finally happens, he is overwhelmed by the majesty and splendour of the Lord. As Elihu said, to meet God is like looking into the sun. When the glory of the Lord is revealed, we are safer to look away. Job thought he had much to say but finds he has lost his words.

In question after question, God itemises his wisdom and power in creation (38:1—39:30). Who else could create such wonders? Can a mere human understand how it all works? Can Job explain such marvels, let alone reproduce them? Is he the creator or simply a creature? Is he God or a mere mortal?

Notice that God does not focus on either Job's sinfulness or his innocence. The issue is whether or not he is qualified to question God's justice and challenge his ways: 'Will the one who contends with the Almighty correct him? Let him who accuses God answer him!' (40:2). Having been put so firmly in his place, Job at least has the wisdom to say no more.

We do well to cultivate a similar humility and to remember our own smallness. Tiny human minds can never fathom all the ways of God, especially when it comes to suffering. Sometimes we will need to be content with not knowing and choose to trust in God's goodness rather than our human wisdom.

Lord, I bow before your greatness. You alone are God.

TONY HORSFALL

Eating humble pie

'I know that you can do all things; no purpose of yours can be thwarted. You asked, "Who is this that obscures my plans without knowledge?" Surely I spoke of things I did not understand, things too wonderful for me to know. You said, "Listen now, and I will speak; I will question you, and you shall answer me." My ears had heard of you but now my eyes have seen you. Therefore I despise myself and repent in dust and ashes.'

All the way through, Job has protested his innocence and arrogantly asserted that he knows better than God, bringing God's justice into question. In order to defend his own integrity, he has maligned God. Now he realises the error of his ways.

Job had been rendered silent by his encounter with the Almighty, and now his silence is turned to repentance. He acknowledges that he was out of his depth, speaking of things he knew nothing about. His intellectual arrogance has been exposed and he sees for himself his own pride. His repentance is deep and sincere.

Job was a righteous man who feared God and did what was right, but his understanding of God was primarily in his mind, not his heart. He knew about God but did not *know* God until this moment of encounter, and it floored him. God humbled him without humiliating him. This first-hand knowledge of God changed him completely: 'My ears had heard of you, but now my eyes have seen you' (v. 5).

Encounter is a prerequisite for spiritual growth. We do not know God simply by reading about him or listening to others talk about him. We have to meet him for ourselves. Such an encounter will inevitably make us more self-aware, especially of our own humanity and smallness. He is the creator; we are his creatures. Only when such humility is firmly established within us can we begin to understand God and his ways.

Furthermore, knowing he is sovereign, and submitting to his will for our lives, keeps us walking in his ways. We may not always understand what he is doing but we can trust him to do what is right.

Lord, grant me an insight into your majesty. Help me to trust you more.

TONY HORSFALL

Restoration

After Job had prayed for his friends, the Lord restored his fortunes and gave him twice as much as he had before. All his brothers and sisters and everyone who had known him before came and ate with him in his house. They comforted and consoled him over all the trouble the Lord had brought on him, and each one gave him a piece of silver and a gold ring. The Lord blessed the latter part of Job's life more than the former part.

The circle is complete again when the Lord restores Job's fortunes and blesses him in even greater measure than before. Yet this is not a return to the status quo. Things are fundamentally different.

Job understands now that his good fortune is not a matter of reward for obedience. Having encountered God and realised his own folly and pride, he knows such favour is undeserved. It is a gift of grace to be received humbly and with thanksgiving. Job had responded to God in repentance without any promise of restored blessing. That such abundance followed was a bonus.

In this way Satan's initial question is answered: 'Does Job fear God for nothing?' (1:9). Job has shown by his perseverance that his faith in God is not based on what he gets from God, since when it is all taken away and when he himself is afflicted, he continues to believe. Yes, it is possible for a human being to love God for God's own sake.

Admittedly, at times he is angry with God and questions his justice, but he does not stop believing. Even in the darkness, he had a glimmer of hope: 'But he knows the way I take; when he has tested me, I shall come forth as gold' (23:10). Job has been through the fires and experienced the furnace of affliction, and he has come out of it a better person with a deeper faith.

Perhaps that is the major truth to take from this book. We may not fully understand why we suffer but we can believe that God will somehow use it for our good and his glory.

Lord, I offer my suffering to you. Use it for your glory, for my growth and for the blessing of others.

TONY HORSFALL

The four last things: hell

Most of us, when the subject of hell is mentioned, want to shy away from such an uncomfortable topic – and I have to say that, when asked by the editor to write a series of reflections on the subject, my initial response was to respectfully decline. After all, while the idea of hell is part of the theological (conservative, evangelical, Presbyterian) background to which I belong, it is not an especially prominent theme. I don't recall hearing (or indeed preaching!) many sermons on it, nor claim any particular interest or expertise in the issue.

Hell is a controversial subject: to some, the notion of hell is offensive or cruel; many hold that the afterlife will be a positive experience for everyone. However, if we go to the recorded words of Jesus, is it honest or balanced to accept his statements about heaven, while choosing to ignore or reject those concerning hell?

Within Christian traditions, there are a variety of views and theological fashions change. Even among the early church fathers, there was tension: Augustine saw hell as eternal torment; Irenaeus favoured annihilationism; Origen supported universalism. Each of these views has found serious theological support and been regarded as orthodox at some stage in the history of the church. Many argue that none of these views should be lightly or thoughtlessly dismissed, regarding ambiguity in the text of scripture as deliberate, with a divinely intended effect on our obedience.

Some resources I have found helpful include John Blanchard's brief *The Truth about Hell* and Jonathan Edwards' classic sermon 'Sinners in the hands of an angry God'. A special mention, too, to my 13-year-old son, James, who, in seeing me wresting with this topic, bought me Ajith Fernando's *Crucial Questions about Hell* as a Father's Day gift.

The next two weeks will not always be comfortable. Some of what will be discussed you may disagree with; we will touch on some areas that I hope will make you think. But my prayer is that you will be drawn closer to God, and that God will gain glory. As Rob Bell has said, 'A good sermon is going to disturb the comfortable and comfort the disturbed. It inspires you. It provokes you. It should make your soul soar.'

MURDO MACDONALD

Sheol

'But a man dies and is laid low; he breathes his last and is no more... so he lies down and does not rise; till the heavens are no more, people will not awake or be roused from their sleep. If only you would hide me in the grave and conceal me till your anger has passed! If only you would set me a time and then remember me! If someone dies, will they live again? All the days of my hard service I will wait for my renewal to come.'

The Hebrew word *sheol* (translated as 'grave' in today's passage) is sometimes rendered in English translations of the Bible as 'hell'. Ancient near eastern cultures (including Israel) viewed the world very differently from how we do. Three (normally separate) realms were envisaged: the heavens, where the gods dwelt; earth, inhabited by the living; and the underworld, where all who had died resided. In scripture, Sheol usually refers to this third realm.

Sheol was seen as the destination of all who died, with little judgement or differentiation between those who lived righteous or unrighteous lives. King David on his deathbed spoke of being 'about to go the way of all the earth' (1 Kings 2:2). Rather than facing consequences in an afterlife, judgement and punishment were expected to be meted out during a person's lifetime.

However, many of us know all too painfully that life isn't always like that: as many psalms reflect, too often the wicked prosper while those who are faithful face challenges. How can a righteous person facing terrible circumstances make sense of their situation? We can be encouraged that, in today's passage, even in the face of seeming futility and frustration of life, Job ends with a note of hope, as he waits for renewal to come.

While the concepts associated with Sheol in the Old Testament are somewhat different to those which we, living in the light of the New Testament revelation, would normally link to hell, with Job we can take comfort that God is in control.

Perhaps you, or someone known to you, are facing fear and frustration, lacking hope. Pray for the Holy Spirit to renew and refresh you or them.

MURDO MACDONALD

Gehenna

'You have heard that it was said to the people long ago, "You shall not murder, and anyone who murders will be subject to judgement." But I tell you that anyone who is angry with a brother or sister will be subject to judgement. Again, anyone who says to a brother or sister, "Raca," is answerable to the court. And anyone who says, "You fool!" will be in danger of the fire of hell.'

The New Testament word most often translated into English as 'hell' is the Greek 'Gehenna'. The word originally referred to a valley on the outskirts of Jerusalem that was associated with evil practices, including human sacrifice (Jeremiah 7:31). It eventually became a public dump, where rubbish, offal, bodies of dead animals and executed criminals were flung. Jesus' original hearers would know it as a place of great unpleasantness, fire and danger – not somewhere you would want to spend a lot of time.

In developing countries today, many people are forced by circumstance to literally live on the rubbish and detritus of others. I remember feeling unsafe and unwelcome (by both human inhabitants and marauding hyenas) on an ill-judged night-time visit to one such site in Ethiopia.

By Jesus' time, the view that death was followed by resurrection, to either reward or punishment, was widely held. This parallels the idea of a kingdom – initially this was seen as an earthly, physical kingdom, based around Jerusalem, but following the exile, this also took on a spiritual nature.

The gospels record Jesus using the term 'Gehenna' eleven times, often indicating a place of exclusion and banishment – the opposite to life in the kingdom, which he offers (e.g. Mark 9:43–48). The idea of the kingdom of God is especially prominent in the gospel of Matthew: there are those who are seen as being 'in the kingdom' and those who are 'outside' the kingdom.

The concepts invoked by Jesus in referencing Gehenna act to warn and reproach – a spiritual 'Danger – keep out' sign. We always do well to heed warnings of dangers that lie ahead.

We perhaps find it easy to consider some people 'outside' the kingdom. Jesus makes it clear that he came to seek and save those who were lost.

MURDO MACDONALD

Hades

His face was like the sun shining in all its brilliance. When I saw him, I fell at his feet as though dead. Then he placed his right hand on me and said: 'Do not be afraid. I am the First and the Last. I am the Living One; I was dead, and now look, I am alive forever and ever! And I hold the keys of death and Hades. Write, therefore, what you have seen, what is now and what will take place later.

The Greek translation of the Old Testament, known as the Septuagint, translated the Hebrew word *sheol* as 'Hades'– a term borrowed from Greek mythology, denoting a concept similar to the limbo of the unjudged dead of Sheol. Greek thought had also begun to develop an idea of eternal punishment – a realm of Hades known as Tartarus, more similar to the idea of hell that we often imagine (2 Peter 2:4).

Hades is used in a scattering of passages in the New Testament, and typically implies neither fire nor punishment but forgottenness. Its use on a number of occasions in the apocalyptic vision of Revelation perhaps suggests that death and forgottenness will themselves be destroyed, when both death and Hades are cast into the lake of fire at what is termed 'the second death' (Revelation 20:14). This in turn ties in with the idea of death being 'the last enemy to be destroyed' (1 Corinthians 15:26), when Christ hands the kingdom over to God the Father.

Many of us are haunted by what has happened to us in our past. Perhaps that very destruction of the ability to forget, to put behind us past failures and negative experiences, is one aspect of what makes the prospect of hell so awful. However, we can give thanks that God has promised that, in Christ, our sins are forgiven and forgotten, and 'as far as the east is from the west, so far has he removed our transgressions from us' (Psalm 103:12).

'Rock of Ages, cleft for me, let me hide myself in Thee; let the water and the blood, from Thy riven side which flowed, be of sin the double cure, cleanse me from its guilt and power' (A.M. Toplady, 1740–78).

MURDO MACDONALD

Sin

We were by nature deserving of wrath. But because of his great love for us, God, who is rich in mercy, made us alive with Christ even when we were dead in transgressions – it is by grace you have been saved. And God raised us up with Christ and seated us with him in the heavenly realms in Christ Jesus, in order that in the coming ages he might show the incomparable riches of his grace, expressed in his kindness to us in Christ Jesus. For it is by grace you have been saved, through faith – and this is not from yourselves, it is the gift of God – not by works, so that no one can boast.

My nephew, while training as a minister, was reprimanded for saying in a sermon that people were sinful; people don't like being reminded of their failings, his supervisor reasoned.

The subject of sin, its consequences and how to deal with it, is rarely far from the surface in scripture. From disobedience in the garden of Eden, through the need for Old Testament sacrificial offerings to atone for wrong-doing, our humanity is depicted as being persistently and unavoidably tainted with sin.

However unpopular the subject, thinking about hell means we must consider sin and its consequences. In his teachings, Jesus is often recorded as talking about sin and judgement; Paul reminds the faithful in Ephesus that our sinfulness means that, while God loves us, in our natural state, we are 'by nature deserving of wrath' (Ephesians 2:3).

My nephew's tutor was right: nobody likes to be reminded of their short-comings. However, we cannot simply ignore this elephant in the room and hope it goes away. God certainly doesn't! The glory of the gospel is that, by the perfect sacrifice of Christ, 'once for sins, the righteous for the unright-eous, to bring you to God' (1 Peter 3:18), God by his grace has opened the way for us through faith in Christ to move from death to life.

As the writer to the Hebrews puts it, 'How shall we escape if we ignore so great a salvation?' (Hebrews 2:3).

Give thanks to God for the salvation from sin and wrongdoing,
which has been bought for us by the sacrifice of Christ.

MURDO MACDONALD

Condemned

For God so loved the world that he gave his one and only Son, that whoever believes in him shall not perish but have eternal life. For God did not send his Son into the world to condemn the world, but to save the world through him. Whoever believes in him is not condemned, but whoever does not believe stands condemned already because they have not believed in the name of God's one and only Son.

To many, the passage before us contains the ultimate expression of the gospel; John 3:16 is certainly one of the most quoted verses in the Bible, and with good reason, as it explains in a nutshell that God reaches out in love to those who need salvation.

We are often guilty, however, of taking verse 16 out of context; the allusion in verse 14 to the lifting up of the snake in the desert points forward to Christ's crucifixion – but also back to a past occasion when God acted to bring good out of terrible circumstances (see Numbers 21:8–9). I am reminded of Mysani, a long-term resident of the Nepalese Leprosy Mission hospital we worked in for a decade, who would often thank God for her leprosy, as it meant that, in seeking treatment from the hospital, she encountered the gospel of Christ.

We also sometimes fail to give adequate attention to the subsequent statement of Jesus in verse 18 – that the ultimate, just destiny for all, without the gracious intervention of God in salvation, is condemnation. In other words, we are all naturally hell-bound. Failure to acknowledge the lordship of Christ means that we remain under condemnation for our sins.

Hudson Taylor, the pioneer missionary to China, is famously quoted as saying, 'Christ is either Lord of all, or is not Lord at all.' I recall one of my good friends from university pointing out that some will bow the knee to Christ willingly, some unwillingly – but ultimately *all* will bow (Philippians 2:10).

'There are only two kinds of people in the end: those who say to God, "Thy will be done," and those to whom God says, in the end, "Thy will be done"' (C.S. Lewis, 1898–1963).

MURDO MACDONALD

Imprisoned

'Then the master called the servant in. "You wicked servant," he said…
"Shouldn't you have had mercy on your fellow servant just as I had on
you?" In anger his master handed him over to the jailers to be tortured,
until he should pay back all he owed. This is how my heavenly Father
will treat each of you unless you forgive your brother or sister from your
heart.'

On a train journey once, I got chatting to a submariner, and so learned
about an aspect of our country's defence to which most of us give little
thought. Having, as a young boy, once been on a tour of a naval submarine
visiting Stornoway, I had some sense of the claustrophobic nature of such
a vessel. This man and his 130 colleagues would spend up to 18 months
on a voyage – constantly underwater – with little contact with the outside
world as communications risked the possibility of adversaries detecting
the position of their nuclear-armed vessel.

While not imprisonment in the conventional sense, being under the
sea for a year and a half with dozens of others in a tube 12m in diameter
and 150m long doesn't fill me (or indeed my travelling companion that
day) with a great sense of enjoyment – imagine the mental, physical and
emotional effects.

While most of us will have little experience of physical imprisonment,
as I write, in spring 2020, many around the world are in lockdown, largely
confined to our homes as a response to the coronavirus pandemic. This has
meant isolation and loneliness for many – and, much as we love our families, some of us are realising it is possible to get too much of a good thing!

The image of imprisonment is one which is used on a number of occasions in scripture in relation to hell. Prisons in biblical times would have
been places of great horror, and would have included physical punishment
or abuse as well as the limitations on personal liberty with which we now
associate them. As the hellish nature of imprisonment would not be lost
on Jesus' original hearers, so we too can take warning.

Pray for people who may feel trapped or imprisoned
by their current circumstances.

MURDO MACDONALD

Fire

'**The beggar died and the angels carried him to Abraham's side. The rich man also died and was buried. In Hades, where he was in torment, he looked up and saw Abraham far away, with Lazarus by his side. So he called to him, "Father Abraham, have pity on me and send Lazarus to dip the tip of his finger in water and cool my tongue, because I am in agony in this fire."'**

If there is one word associated most closely with hell, it is surely 'fire'; Jesus spoke of a place where 'the fire is not quenched' (Mark 9:48), and in this, the only recorded story of Jesus that contains named characters, the rich man is depicted as having had a life of ease, while Lazarus begged at his gate. After death, the rich man finds himself in Hades, conscious of his surroundings and sufferings, of what has gone before and of the alternate state of being 'in the bosom of Abraham', which Lazarus is now enjoying.

This vivid story, which is almost literally burned on our memory, warns of the consequences of refusal to listen to Moses and the prophets (Luke 16:31). Jesus' rising from death opens the door to coming of the kingdom, when all wrongs will be put right.

Throughout scripture, fire is closely associated with the holiness of God – think, for example, of the consuming fire of God at the dedication of Solomon's temple (2 Chronicles 7:1) and the tongues of fire coming at Pentecost in Acts 2.

While we often picture hell as a handing over by God to be subjected to fire controlled by Satan, the enemy of God, it has been argued that what scripture seeks to convey may be that, rather than being indicative of his absence, the fire of hell represents God's inescapable holy eternal presence.

How we behave matters. While God is ultimately in control, our responsibility, as Paul reminds us, is to 'build with care. For… the fire will test the quality of each person's work' (1 Corinthians 3:10–13).

'I sometimes think of hell as a terrible burning within our hearts for God, to fellowship with God, a fire that we can never quench'
(Billy Graham, 1918–2018).

MURDO MACDONALD

Light and darkness

'Death is swallowed up in victory.' 'O Death, where *is* your sting? O Hades, where *is* your victory?' The sting of death *is* sin, and the strength of sin *is* the law. But thanks *be* to God, who gives us the victory through our Lord Jesus Christ. Therefore, my beloved brethren, be steadfast, immovable, always abounding in the work of the Lord, knowing that your labour is not in vain in the Lord.

Fire and darkness are two characteristics of hell depicted in the Bible. Many argue that, interpreted literally, these factors conflict. If it is necessary to view at least one of them symbolically, perhaps other descriptions of hell in scripture should also be seen as symbols?

One of the problems is that, when talking about concepts around eternity (heaven as well as hell), we are straining at the limits of what language is able to describe. Perhaps counterintuitively, science sometimes holds that issues which may seem to be mutually exclusive or contradictory are not necessarily so. For example, physicists can show that quantum superposition means that an electron can be in more than one place at once! No, I don't understand it either, but we're not alone in being confused; as physicist Niels Bohr said, 'Anyone not shocked by quantum mechanics has not yet understood it.'

Moses heard the voice of God speaking 'out of the darkness, while the mountain was ablaze with fire' (Deuteronomy 5:23, NIV); Job talks about the land of gloom 'where even the light is like darkness' (Job 10:22, NIV). Such apparently contradictory images of light and darkness stretch our minds even more than quantum mechanics.

Jesus talks about people being cast into outer darkness (Matthew 8:12; 22:13). In any consideration of the matter of hell, we must not lose sight of the fact that, for all the darkness and gloom of the subject, the glorious vision of heaven is also before us. God is described as being light (1 John 1:5), and through Christ we have the opportunity to live in the presence of the perfect light. We rejoice that in Christ, as Paul reminds us, death is swallowed up in victory.

Give thanks that God is able to shine a light into even the darkest gloom.

MURDO MACDONALD

Weeping and gnashing of teeth

'His master replied, "You wicked, lazy servant! So you knew that I harvest where I have not sown and gather where I have not scattered seed? Well then, you should have put my money on deposit with the bankers, so that when I returned I would have received it back with interest… And throw that worthless servant outside, into the darkness, where there will be weeping and gnashing of teeth."'

More than half of Jesus' 40 recorded parables contain references to judgement; clearly, it is a teaching that Jesus was keen to get across. In Matthew 24 and 25, Jesus discourses on judgement, including two parables on the nature of the kingdom of God ushered in by this. Jesus concludes the second parable with these verses, then moves on to the idea of a day of reckoning, when the unrighteous will 'go away to eternal punishment, but the righteous to eternal life' (Matthew 25:46).

Most of us have experienced examinations, whether A levels, driving tests or job interviews. While we often view this scene as depicting a kind of cosmic examination, Jesus' emphasis is on the servant who is cast into tortured outer darkness as a consequence of failure to follow the master's instructions.

The term 'gnashing of teeth' seems to have been a favourite of Matthew; all but one of the seven utterances of the phrase by Jesus are found in his gospel. The context in which it is used has lead to this image of repentant weeping and an agonised physical response being closely associated with hell.

Weeping is more than simply crying; it describes tears of terrible grief, triggered by many factors, including the shame of experiencing the anger of a righteous God. Gnashing of teeth is used in scripture as a way of expressing anger (e.g. Acts 7:54); in this context, the anger may be directed at the realisation of what might have been or anger at God for his condemnation.

Repentance is a key part of what it means to be a follower of Christ. Give thanks that 'if we confess our sins, he is faithful and just and will forgive us our sins and purify us from all unrighteousness' (1 John 1:9).

MURDO MACDONALD

God of love, holiness and justice

I saw the Lord, high and exalted, seated on a throne; and the train of his robe filled the temple… 'Holy, holy, holy is the Lord Almighty; the whole earth is full of his glory'… the doorposts and thresholds shook and the temple was filled with smoke. 'Woe to me!' I cried. 'I am ruined! For I am a man of unclean lips, and I live among a people of unclean lips, and my eyes have seen the King, the Lord Almighty.'

How can a God who is love possibly condemn anyone to hell? If love is central to the character of God, he has it within his power to overlook all wrongdoing, to forgive and to welcome all into his eternal presence. If God is truly a God of love and grace, why is any divine punishment required at all? As German poet Henrich Heine (1797–1856) put it, 'God will forgive; that is his job.' However, to reduce the Lord of all glory to a mere functionary who carries out tasks on our behalf is to surely misunderstand our relationship with our creator.

This question is one with which theologians have wrestled for millennia; we cannot pretend that this is an easy dilemma to resolve. While many hold on to the essential characteristic of God that we find most attractive – his love for us – we need to balance that with other aspects of his character that are revealed in scripture, such as those of justice and holiness.

In his vision, Isaiah was made aware that the demand could not be higher – God is holy. Our predicament could not be greater – sinners cannot possibly be this holy. Yet the Father's answer could not be more gracious – his Son died in our place to satisfy his need for holiness, making him able to forgive without forsaking his own righteousness.

God's love isn't like our fluctuating emotions nor is it a sloppy sentimentalism that brushes aside all shortcomings; it is part of his unchanging and eternal nature. While we give thanks that God is gracious and loving, we do well to remember that he is also holy and just.

'There is nothing that keeps wicked men at any one moment out of hell, but the mere pleasure of God' (Jonathan Edwards, 1703–58).

MURDO MACDONALD

Annihilation?

'Do not be afraid of those who kill the body but cannot kill the soul. Rather, be afraid of the One who can destroy both soul and body in hell… Whoever acknowledges me before others, I will also acknowledge before my Father in heaven. But whoever disowns me before others, I will disown before my Father in heaven. Do not suppose that I have come to bring peace to the earth. I did not come to bring peace, but a sword.'

Some argue that, while they may be real, punishment and hell are conditional states. This has led to the idea that while those who go to heaven are in an everlasting state of fellowship with God, existence in hell is in some sense temporary, an approach known as annihilationism.

Many proponents of this view accept that God is just, so some punishment for sinful behaviour is necessary. However, as God is also merciful, punishing a person for all eternity for sins that were committed over a few decades of life on earth is disproportionate. At some point, the souls of those condemned to punishment cease to exist – they are annihilated. Having received punishment for sinfulness, they suffer no more.

Supporters of this view point to Bible passages such as this or 1 Thessalonians 5:3, which talk about the 'destruction' of the wicked, arguing that, in the end, those who have consistently disobeyed will be destroyed. This appears to satisfy God's justice and wrath but avoids the problem of him appearing to be a spiteful despot who metes out unnecessarily harsh punishment.

The most often repeated command in scripture (included three times in this section) is 'do not be afraid'. While we may be buffeted by life's circumstances, ultimately, as Jesus reminds us here, God is the righteous judge into whose hands we can, without fear, place all things.

'To enter heaven is to become more human than you ever succeeded in being on earth; to enter hell is to be banished from humanity. What is cast (or casts itself) into hell is not a man: it is "remains." To be a complete man means to have the passions obedient to the will and the will offered to God' (C.S. Lewis).

MURDO MACDONALD

Evangelism

Jesus… said to him, 'Zacchaeus, come down immediately. I must stay at your house today.' So he came down at once and welcomed him gladly. All the people saw this and began to mutter, 'He has gone to be the guest of a sinner'… Jesus said to him, 'Today salvation has come to this house, because this man, too, is a son of Abraham. For the Son of Man came to seek and to save the lost.'

We all love Zacchaeus. As an example of successful evangelism, he's hard to beat. Everybody in town knew the little tax collector was a sinner, yet Jesus had no hesitation in dining with him – and in declaring him saved.

One of the questions that repeatedly comes up in discussions around hell is its place in evangelism. Is it appropriate to invoke the threat of punishment, in order to entice (or frighten) people into following the way of Christ? As well as holding out the prospect of eternal life in the presence of God, Jesus had no hesitation in talking about judgement and hell. But should we also be using it?

Our motives, even in seeking to share the good news of the gospel, are sometimes skewed by our fallen nature (as the apostle Paul reminds us Philippians 1). While we must always be mindful of our nature, we can also be assured that, as we share the message of Christ, we are following his example if we also make people aware of the consequences of not taking the gospel seriously.

Jesus makes it clear that he came to seek and save the lost, and God's Holy Spirit 'will convict the world of sin, and of righteousness, and of judgement' (John 16:8, NKJV). While not our primary motivation in evangelism, the terrible prospect of hell can surely have a place as we seek to share the good news.

'If sinners will be damned, at least let them leap to hell over our bodies. And if they will perish, let them perish with our arms around their knees, imploring them to stay. If hell must be filled, at least let it be filled in the teeth of our exertions, and let not one go there unwarned and unprayed for' (C.H. Spurgeon, 1834–92).

MURDO MACDONALD

Dante's inferno and other imaginings

'If anyone worships the beast and its image and receives its mark on their forehead or on their hand, they, too, will drink the wine of God's fury, which has been poured full strength into the cup of his wrath. They will be tormented with burning sulphur in the presence of the holy angels and of the Lamb. And the smoke of their torment will rise forever and ever. There will be no rest day or night for those who worship the beast and its image, or for anyone who receives the mark of its name.' This calls for patient endurance on the part of the people of God who keep his commands and remain faithful to Jesus.

Perhaps the most famous work of the 14th-century Italian poet Dante is his *Divine Comedy*, which includes his lurid vision of Inferno. Dante pictured hell as a vast, cone-shaped pit, concentric circles of torment reaching down to the centre of the earth.

Images such as these have been picked up by artists and writers in an attempt to convey the depravity of hell. For many, including Christians, similarly graphic depictions of the terrors and tortures of hell have been more instrumental than scripture in shaping the images we have of hell.

Powerful though some of these imaginings may be, we must remember that, beyond some brief depictions, such as the one in these verses, there is strikingly little detail in scripture on what hell (or indeed heaven, for that matter) may be like. As in this passage, the focus in scripture is often on the fact that God reigns, that he is coming in salvation and that his victory will be just, thorough and complete.

While giving us warning glimpses of what is to come, God, in his grace, shields us from the full force of much of what is beyond even our wildest imaginings.

'It is unwise for Christians to claim any knowledge of either the furniture of heaven or the temperature of hell; or to be too certain about any details of the Kingdom of God in which history is consummated. But it is prudent to accept the testimony of the heart, which affirms the fear of judgment'
(Reinhold Niebuhr, 1892–1971).

MURDO MACDONALD

Descended into hell

For Christ also suffered once for sins, the righteous for the unrighteous, to bring you to God. He was put to death in the body but made alive in the Spirit. After being made alive, he went and made proclamation to the imprisoned spirits – to those who were disobedient long ago when God waited patiently in the days of Noah while the ark was being built.

Many of us will use a creed on a regular basis, perhaps as part of our liturgy. Generally positive statements of accepted doctrine, the creeds were designed as aides-memoire to remind Christians of what they believe.

The Apostles Creed appeared in its original form in the third century AD and was widely adopted across the western church. The wording used by both the Roman Catholic Church and the Church of England (in the 1662 Book of Common Prayer) contains the statement (based on the verses before us) that Christ 'descended into hell'. Reciting this phrase is probably the occasion many of us most frequently hear or use the word 'hell'!

In what sense could the holy Son of God have entered what is seen as the epitome of evil? Throughout his earthy life, Jesus was in fellowship with his heavenly Father. However, in the garden of Gethsemane we see him wrestling with the awfulness of the experience he is about to go through yet, in faithfulness, praying, 'Yet not as I will, but as you will' (Matthew 26:39). On the cross, Jesus cried out that he had been forsaken by his father (Matthew 27:46), and with this cry his earthly life ended. To those observing, a promising mission had ended in failure: Christ, a good man who lived an exemplary life and taught many commendable behaviours and principles, was ultimately, as Mary Magdalene sings in *Jesus Christ Superstar*, 'just a man'.

But, unlike the musical, the story of Jesus Christ doesn't end with the cross: his resurrection showed his victory over death and hell. While we may not yet fully understand it, we live our lives in the light of this victory.

---

*'Tis mystery all, the immortal dies. Who can explain his strange design…
No condemnation now I dread, Jesus and all in him is mine'
(Charles Wesley, 1707–88).*

MURDO MACDONALD

Zechariah

When thinking about my upcoming writing projects, I knew I would be writing on Zechariah. Our editor commissions these notes ahead of time, so my memory of the details of the project grew hazy, and I anticipated the challenge of digging into the story of one of the Old Testament prophets. But then I realised that I was to write about Zechariah, father of John the Baptist – which made much more sense with these notes falling at the beginning of Advent.

I think you'll enjoy and benefit from this fortnight of exploring his story as we prepare ourselves to celebrate the birth of Jesus. Zechariah plays an important role in ushering in God's plan of salvation. Yet his journey has bumps along the road, and we can probably relate to his questioning of God over a promised gift because he didn't have enough faith to believe that God would follow through. But we can be encouraged by Zechariah's response once he endures God's discipline of silence – he bursts forth in praise of the living God.

Sticking with reading these notes as we enter the busy days of December can help you to resist the cultural bent towards celebrating Christmas during Advent. For many, instead of this time being a period of self-reflection and getting ready, it can be over-filled with holiday lunches, Christmas parties and the frenetic activity of shopping and planning. For many, the season can feel overwhelming and lacking in joy. But as we set aside time to read the Bible and pray, we can open ourselves to God's working in our lives – even if our days are still full of activity.

I'm grateful for the range of Bible commentaries that I consulted on Luke's gospel, for the wisdom of those steeped in the original language and culture. I consulted several, but received the most help from the Luke scholar Darrell Bock in his *Baker Exegetical Commentary on the New Testament* (Baker, 1994) and the *NIV Application Commentary: Luke* (Zondervan, 1996).

May you be surprised by God during these weeks as he reveals himself to you, perhaps even with a special commission, as you prepare for the joy of his Son being born again in our lives.

AMY BOUCHER PYE

A careful account

Many have undertaken to draw up an account of the things that have been fulfilled among us, just as they were handed down to us by those who from the first were eye witnesses and servants of the word. With this in mind, since I myself have carefully investigated everything from the beginning, I too decided to write an orderly account for you, most excellent Theophilus, so that you may know the certainty of the things you have been taught.

Imagine what the run-up to Christmas would look like if we didn't have Luke's gospel. We'd not get to enjoy nativity plays with the innkeeper proclaiming, 'There's no room at the inn', or the shepherds crowding in to celebrate the birth of the Saviour. And we'd not know about the revelation to Zechariah from the angel Gabriel about his wife in their old age bearing a son, John, the messenger who would prepare the way for Jesus.

Luke has given us a gift with his accounts in the New Testament, not only his gospel but the book of Acts. As the author of these two, he penned more of the New Testament than anyone else (and the book of Luke is the longest by way of the number of words in the New Testament). Although he wasn't an eyewitness to Jesus, he had access to first-hand accounts and is recognised as Paul's companion in many of his missionary journeys.

Luke was a Gentile writing for the Gentiles, the only contributor to the Bible who wasn't Jewish. He was careful to put together a trustworthy account, because he wants Theophilus, who may have been his benefactor, to have a strong and robust faith in God through Christ. As a physician who had undergone training, Luke would have brought his skills of observation and application to his writing of the gospel – combined with, of course, the inspiration of the Holy Spirit. With his account, we can more fully prepare ourselves to celebrate the birth of Jesus.

Creator God, thank you for the way you made us in your image, imparting us with wisdom and knowledge. Help us to honour you as we prepare for Jesus' birth and increase our love for you.

AMY BOUCHER PYE

Righteous before God

In the time of Herod king of Judea there was a priest named Zechariah, who belonged to the priestly division of Abijah; his wife Elizabeth was also a descendant of Aaron. Both of them were righteous in the sight of God, observing all the Lord's commands and decrees blamelessly. But they were childless because Elizabeth was not able to conceive, and they were both very old.

Four hundred years must have felt like a long time for God's people not to receive any words of revelation from him. In the last Old Testament book, Malachi, God promised, 'I will send my messenger, who will prepare the way before me' (Malachi 3:1), but generation after generation died without seeing the fulfilment of this promise. But then came Zechariah and Elizabeth, whom Luke names as faithful people who followed God's commands. To Zechariah would God break his long silence with the promise of this messenger.

In the ancient Near East, people would assume that those who weren't parents must have sinned to keep God from giving them the gift of children. Luke, however, emphasises that this couple are not only upstanding but those who observed the law without fault. That they had no children did not reflect their standing before God. Indeed, God would change Elizabeth from barren to fertile, even in her old age. He blessed them richly with a son who would play a key role in welcoming the salvation of the world.

When our plans are scuppered, we might be tempted to blame God or think of him as silent and uncaring. But we lack God's perspective and cannot know all of the factors at play. Perhaps he will redeem our broken dreams in mind-blowing ways, like he did for Elizabeth and Zechariah. Or maybe his work will include mending our hearts and bringing healing and hope, even if our circumstances do not change. If we're in a place of disappointment, we can trust that our heavenly Father cares deeply for us.

Loving Lord, you brought great joy to Zechariah and Elizabeth after years of heartache. Give me hope and strengthen my faith in you, for I know that you are good and that you care for me.

AMY BOUCHER PYE

Perfect timing

Once when Zechariah's division was on duty and he was serving as priest before God, he was chosen by lot, according to the custom of the priesthood, to go into the temple of the Lord and burn incense. And when the time for the burning of incense came, all the assembled worshippers were praying outside. Then an angel of the Lord appeared to him, standing at the right side of the altar of incense.

A popular meme shows up on social media about God's timing, that he's never early, never late, but always on time. We might, if we're feeling left out, overlooked or bruised from disappointment, want to quibble with the sentiment. After all, we live in a fallen world in which we will encounter tragedy and sadness. But I appreciate the thought behind the saying in terms of how it points to God's loving providence. For although we will experience many difficult things, he *will* work according to his wisdom and perfect timing in our lives. And this is what we see at play in today's reading.

Zechariah was a priest serving in the temple, one of about 18,000 priests. We might guess that he would often burn the incense there, but actually this was a once-in-a-lifetime occurrence as he only would serve in the temple for two one-week periods each year. The special honour of burning the incense was chosen by lot, a means of selection that God often used, such as before he gave the Holy Spirit to believers at Pentecost. Clearly the Lord wanted to use this special moment of Zechariah worshipping him to deliver his message of good news.

During this time of Advent, as we prepare our hearts to welcome anew the presence of the Lord, why not pause before God and ask him to help you understand his timing in your life. As you look back over the past year, ask for wisdom to understand not only the challenges you faced but the triumphs and joys too. As we discern God's hand in the little and big things, our faith in him will grow stronger.

Lord Jesus, you humbled yourself to become a human being, one of us.
Thank you for making this sacrifice of love.

AMY BOUCHER PYE

Answered prayers

When Zechariah saw him, he was startled and was gripped with fear. But the angel said to him: 'Do not be afraid, Zechariah; your prayer has been heard. Your wife Elizabeth will bear you a son, and you are to call him John. He will be a joy and delight to you, and many will rejoice because of his birth, for he will be great in the sight of the Lord.'

God can burst into our lives unexpectedly at any time. Sometimes his work is dramatic and unmissable, but many times his appearance will feel more like a soft whisper, easily overlooked. For Zechariah, God sent an angel whom the priest was not expecting. Zechariah's heart must have pounded at the sight of the angel, for Gabriel's first words were those often uttered by these heavenly beings: 'Don't be afraid.' Gabriel's message was one of shock and delight – Zechariah and Elizabeth would at long last be parents.

Just as the 400 years of silence from God had come to an end, so too would their period of barrenness cease. Elizabeth and Zechariah would follow the example of Abraham and Sarah or of Hannah, the mother of Samuel, who received the gift of a child unexpectedly. The blessing for Zechariah and Elizabeth, as in those cases, would not only be for them as parents with John bringing them joy and delight but for God's people more broadly. Even before John's birth, God promised to bless him and make him great in his sight.

As we ponder this unexpected visit, we can think about welcoming God's presence this Advent as we prepare to celebrate Jesus' presence in our lives. God may choose to visit us through an angel (not something I think I've experienced) or through less dramatic means, such as his Holy Spirit highlighting a passage of the Bible for us. However he chooses to reveal himself, we can make ourselves ready. We can ask him for the faith to believe that he will appear and for the wisdom to discern any divine revelations.

Lord Jesus Christ, Son of the living God, have mercy on me.
Make your home in me and use me to bring you honour
and glory as I share your love with others.

AMY BOUCHER PYE

Filled with the Spirit

'He is never to take wine or other fermented drink, and he will be filled with the Holy Spirit even before he is born. He will bring back many of the people of Israel to the Lord their God.'

The extraordinary appearance of the angel to Zechariah came with an out-of-the-ordinary message – this promised son would have a special mission in God's kingdom. John would follow in the footsteps of the Old Testament priests and prophets who were set apart to do God's work. Because of his special role, he was never to drink alcohol – a prohibition priests respected when they were performing their temple duties, as we see in the law: 'You and your sons are not to drink wine or other fermented drink whenever you go into the tent of meeting' (Leviticus 10:9). His special call would require a life of discipline as he followed God's purposes for his life.

But God would equip him, for John would be filled with the Holy Spirit, even from birth. Later Luke in his narrative details how the Holy Spirit sparked John's recognition of Jesus when they were both in their mother's wombs, for John leaped at Mary's voice (Luke 1:41). John being anointed with the Spirit enabled him to follow and honour God. In this he was a forerunner to all who follow Jesus after Pentecost, when God poured out his Holy Spirit on the believers assembled together. Now we too can enjoy this special status of being set apart for God and filled with his presence.

Advent used to be embraced mainly as a time of fasting to prepare for the feast days of Christmas. Thus it was deemed appropriate to cease from drinking any wine or spirits as people examined their hearts and minds before God, seeking to become right before him. Much of this observance of Advent has been lost today as we enjoy Christmas parties and community gatherings in the run-up to Christmas. Consider cultivating an attitude of preparation and repentance in these days before Christmas, even if you have parties to attend.

Spirit of the living God, fall afresh on me. Mould me and shape me in your image, that I might serve you with joy and consistency.

AMY BOUCHER PYE

Set apart for God

'And he will go on before the Lord, in the spirit and power of Elijah, to turn the hearts of the parents to their children and the disobedient to the wisdom of the righteous – to make ready a people prepared for the Lord.'

Gabriel affirms John's role in the prophetic ministry, saying that he'll follow Elijah in calling people back to God. Note how Gabriel points to the Old Testament precedent of the prophets as he prepares Zechariah for the gift his son will become. As we see from Gabriel's words, John's call is threefold: he will go on before the Lord; he will turn the hearts of the people; he will make them ready. Let's look at each of these.

First, John will go on before the Lord. With the benefit of the gospels, we now recognise how John the Baptist prepared the way for Jesus, calling people to repent and baptising them in the Jordan River. But Zechariah had to believe in faith that his son would take on this role. After so many hundreds of years of silence, would God's promised Messiah really appear?

Second, John will turn the hearts of the people, not only those sinning against God in repentance but those in families who had become separated back to each other. As parents and their children followed different sects, they would grow apart. John's message was that they should unite by following the One who would come after him, who would baptise with 'the Holy Spirit and fire' (Matthew 3:11).

Third, John will make the people ready. He'll follow in the ministry of the prophets in setting apart God's people as they wait for his coming. How soon God would appear in the person of Jesus would have amazed Zechariah.

John had a special role to play in history as the one who came before Jesus, preparing the way for the Messiah. We, of course, won't have that specific task, but we too can gently and sensitively call people to make themselves ready for God's work in their lives.

Lord God, help me to make myself ready for your coming,
that I might reflect your glory as I live for you.

AMY BOUCHER PYE

Doubting God's promise

Zechariah asked the angel, 'How can I be sure of this? I am an old man and my wife is well on in years.' The angel said to him, 'I am Gabriel. I stand in the presence of God, and I have been sent to speak to you and to tell you this good news. And now you will be silent and not able to speak until the day this happens, because you did not believe my words, which will come true at their appointed time.'

I've often wondered why Zechariah is punished for not believing Gabriel's words while Mary, when she questions him about how she can be the mother of Jesus as a virgin, is not reprimanded. Digging into the text with the help of some Bible commentators has helped my understanding.

One main reason lies in Zechariah being a priest who should be well-schooled in the ways of God. Childless couples in their old age receiving the gift of a child is not without precedent, mainly through Abraham and Sarah being given Isaac, the father of Israel. Zechariah seems to overlook them and others from the Old Testament as he queries Gabriel about his message. In doing so, he questions God's ability to work in his life and could be on the way to rejecting the good news the angel brings.

Gabriel is swift to answer. Zechariah's punishment is that he cannot speak throughout Elizabeth's gestation. God will not revoke the promised child, but Zechariah will be rendered silent, unable to share the news of what will happen. He will have plenty of time to ponder the angel's appearance and what will follow.

God still appears in our lives, although not usually in the striking manner as Zechariah experienced. We can choose to welcome him, asking him to help us discern when he is at work, that we might grow in our faith. As we look back, we can often see how he was present with us, whereas at the time it can be harder to discern.

Resurrected Jesus, you live and move in me. Wake me up to the gift of your presence that I might share your love and life with others.

AMY BOUCHER PYE

The Lord's favour

Meanwhile, the people were waiting for Zechariah and wondering why he stayed so long in the temple. When he came out, he could not speak to them. They realised he had seen a vision in the temple, for he kept making signs to them but remained unable to speak. When his time of service was completed, he returned home. After this his wife Elizabeth became pregnant and for five months remained in seclusion. 'The Lord has done this for me,' she said. 'In these days he has shown his favour and taken away my disgrace among the people.'

Zechariah soon understood that what Gabriel promised would indeed come about, for when he finally appeared outside the temple he couldn't speak. The people had been wondering where he was and when he appeared, they realised that he'd experienced something special. But what that was, they weren't to know for many months. Zechariah's inability to speak kept the news from spreading.

Luke doesn't tell us if Zechariah somehow told Elizabeth what happened in the temple or if she received a divine revelation about what was to come. But Luke shares how she points directly to God in thanks after she becomes pregnant. No longer would the women in the village whisper about her barrenness. In her old age, when she thought she was well past her child-bearing years, she would have a baby. We're also not told why Elizabeth keeps herself in seclusion for five months. Perhaps God wanted her to keep her pregnancy a secret, to keep the gossip from spreading.

As followers of Christ, we, like Elizabeth, may be misunderstood. In staying true to God's call for holiness and a whole-hearted commitment to him, we might suffer the gossip of those who don't know our motives. But when we can point to God as the One who brings us joy and fulfils our dreams, we can move past the rejection of those around us. We can stay focused on living to serve him.

Lord, you've done so many amazing things for us. You remove our disgrace and show us your favour. Give us thankful and receptive hearts for your work in our lives.

AMY BOUCHER PYE

Great joy

When it was time for Elizabeth to have her baby, she gave birth to a son. Her neighbours and relatives heard that the Lord had shown her great mercy, and they shared her joy. On the eighth day they came to circumcise the child, and they were going to name him after his father Zechariah, but his mother spoke up and said, 'No! He is to be called John.' They said to her, 'There is no one among your relatives who has that name.'

What must Elizabeth have thought and felt throughout her pregnancy? She, who had been called barren, was with child, and she could feel him moving inside her. God chose to bless her and Zechariah as he set into motion his plans for the birth of his Son, Jesus. The blessing of the nations also included the blessing of this particular family.

A highlight during Elizabeth's pregnancy must have been when her younger cousin Mary came to visit (which we aren't exploring because our focus during this fortnight is on Zechariah). Elizabeth felt great joy over their pregnancies, pronouncing Mary and her child blessed.

And then the long-awaited moment arrived, and Elizabeth gave birth to a son, just as Gabriel had promised. When the neighbours and relatives heard the good news, they were eager to share the couple's joy. But they must have been taken aback when Elizabeth so strongly opposed the naming of the boy after his father, for she knew that John was his name. She wasn't going to acquiesce to peer pressure in going against God's purposes.

Elizabeth weathered the years of pity and scorn, and in her old age received the desires of her heart. She held on to her faith in God and welcomed his work in her life. She probably didn't realise that she would play such a key role in helping to produce the one who would make way for the Lord.

When we say yes to God, we too collaborate with him with effects that we might never even be able to guess.

Creator God, spark your life within me, that I might bring forth your kingdom here on earth. Help me to discern the path I should be taking, for your glory.

AMY BOUCHER PYE

Wonder and awe

Then they made signs to his father, to find out what he would like to name the child. He asked for a writing tablet, and to everyone's astonishment he wrote, 'His name is John.' Immediately his mouth was opened and his tongue set free, and he began to speak, praising God. All the neighbours were filled with awe, and throughout the hill country of Judea people were talking about all these things. Everyone who heard this wondered about it, asking, 'What then is this child going to be?' For the Lord's hand was with him.

In the ancient world, Elizabeth's statement about the naming of John didn't hold enough weight for the concerned family and neighbours, so they enquired of Zechariah. We can infer from the text that Zechariah was probably not only mute but deaf, for the people had to make signs to him to communicate. His answer is an imperative, 'His name *is* John', with the original language conveying the idea that Zechariah had discovered that John had been named accordingly and hadn't done the naming himself.

With that act of obedience, Zechariah is freed from his silence and the first thing he does is to praise God. In his months without speaking, he must have had a long internal dialogue with God about his previous lack of faith. That his speech was restored gave him joy, and he wanted to honour God with his words.

The news spread quickly of not only the unique name of this boy but of Zechariah's restoration. The people began to understand that there was something very special about this baby and the work he was called to do.

If we're stuck in our life with God, part of the reason could be that we've turned from him and not followed through on his commands or direction. When we repent and return to him, we will find the lines of communication restored and a deep joy within.

God of the impossible, work in our lives, our community, our nation.
May your peace and love break through the things that are keeping people
from loving you and each other.

AMY BOUCHER PYE

The horn of salvation

His father Zechariah was filled with the Holy Spirit and prophesied: 'Praise be to the Lord, the God of Israel, because he has come to his people and redeemed them. He has raised up a horn of salvation for us in the house of his servant David (as he said through his holy prophets of long ago).'

Just as Mary, when she met up with Elizabeth, spoke out a hymn of praise to God in thanks for his work of bringing forth salvation through her, so too does Zechariah give praise to God. Like his son, he's filled with the Holy Spirit as he shares his words of adoration. We might be tempted to skim over his song because it forms the last part of John's birth narrative, but actually in that culture its placement at the end gave it more weight and importance.

Zechariah interprets the gift God bestows on his people in terms of the nation of Israel being redeemed. Perhaps he's thinking of the 400 years of silence, with no prophecies or revelations from God, and how now redemption is coming and his people will be set free. The 'horn of salvation' he speaks of implies strength and kingly might, such as the horns of an ox that can help defeat an enemy. But in his song Zechariah also points to the Messiah, the one who, although mighty, will lay down his power and strength in his gracious act of service on the cross.

We can follow Zechariah in praising God after a period of silence when again we sense his voice. We might not fully understand how God has been at work during our time in the fog, but we can trust that he has been bringing about redemption. His love undergirds us and helps us to move forward, even when we feel uncertain about the way ahead.

God of our forebears, thank you for how you moved in and through your people in centuries past, for the prophets and priests who spoke your word and believed you in faith. Spark my heart with love for you and help me to trust you more.

AMY BOUCHER PYE

Serving God without fear

'... salvation from our enemies and from the hand of all who hate us – to show mercy to our ancestors and to remember his holy covenant, the oath he swore to our father Abraham: to rescue us from the hand of our enemies, and to enable us to serve him without fear in holiness and righteousness before him all our days.'

Looking back over our lives, and the lives of those we admire, can help us to discern how God has moved over the years. Even if we feel like his voice is silent for us just now, we can point to his faithfulness and love in times past. We can also consider the heroes of our faith as we seek to trust God with our present and our future. Such as Zechariah did in his song.

He points to God's faithfulness to Abraham, the one recognised as the founder of the faith because of the covenant God made with him. Zechariah reminds God of this covenant of old as he proclaims freedom from their enemies. Again, he has in mind the saving of the nation of Israel.

But then Zechariah moves to action – his gratitude is not simply speaking out words of thanks, but he commits to dedicating his life in the service of God. He wants to live out his gratitude to God as each day he joyfully honours his maker.

To help us in our commitment to God, we can pray through what's known as the examen, a prayer inspired by Ignatius of Loyola. Through it we look back over the day to discern God's movement in our lives. Each night we can think through the day, asking God through his Holy Spirit to bring to mind not only what happened but how we reacted and how God was involved. We can then give thanks or we can offer our sorrow for the ways we let God down. And we can ask God to help us to cling to him the next day.

Comforting Spirit, bring to mind the ways you transform me,
changing me from one who is fearful to one who trusts in you.
Help me to commit to living for you in all my ways each day.

AMY BOUCHER PYE

Light in the darkness

'And you, my child, will be called a prophet of the Most High; for you will go on before the Lord to prepare the way for him, to give his people the knowledge of salvation through the forgiveness of their sins because of the tender mercy of our God, by which the rising sun will come to us from heaven to shine on those living in darkness and in the shadow of death, to guide our feet into the path of peace.'

Zechariah moves from speaking of Israel's salvation to focus on his son. Inspired by the Holy Spirit, he prophesies about John's role in welcoming the Lord, for John will prepare the way for him. John's message will be one of forgiveness of sins when the people repent – a prophecy that came true, as we see in the gospel accounts.

Then Zechariah moves to beautiful language about the light coming in the darkness. Jesus, the rising sun, will dispel the darkness. Because of this light, no longer will the stench of death cling to God's people when they follow the Messiah.

When I think of light shining in the darkness, memories come back to me of being a teenager in the vast wilderness of northern Minnesota, a part of the state that is protected from any development. While camping I would enjoy the star-studded skies on a clear night, but when the clouds would descend, the darkness could feel oppressive. The songs about Jesus being the light would run through my mind as I trekked to the outdoor loo, only able to see a few feet in front of me by the light of the torch as I feared the presence of bears. My application of Jesus as the light of the world was rather specific in that case, but it brought me comfort and peace.

Zechariah's song ends with the statement of God's people walking in peace. This forms the heart of John's message – receive the forgiveness for your sins and enjoy God's peace.

Jesus, the morning star, you light my path. Shine your light in the darkness, dispelling any fear, bitterness and evil. May your people flood their cities with your love and your light.

AMY BOUCHER PYE

Hope in the wilderness

And the child grew and became strong in spirit; and he lived in the wilderness until he appeared publicly to Israel.

We come to the end of John's birth narrative with all of its surprises as God breaks into their lives. A barren couple, past their prime, are given the promise of a son, but the father-to-be doesn't believe the divine promise. His months of seclusion end with his act of obedience, when he responds to God's work with praise as he shares of the amazing things God is doing in their midst. And John grows and becomes strong in spirit through the work of the Holy Spirit.

Note that John lives in the wilderness in his formative years, only appearing to Israel at the appointed time. The wilderness can be a literal or a figurative experience for many in their journey of faith. Many people connect times of hardship and difficulty to being wilderness experiences, where they may not have sensed the presence of God. But in looking back, they can see how they clung to God through the challenges, their faith growing stronger and more robust. Aleksandr Solzhenitsyn hints at this when he says in *The Gulag Archipelago*, 'Bless you prison, bless you for being in my life.' His soul matured through his time when he was locked up.

We might not seek these wilderness experiences, but the desert fathers and mothers actively pursued life in the actual desert for the ways it would bring them closer to God. There they would encounter wild animals, the chilling cold of the night, the scorching heat of the day, hunger and demons. And many people would venture out into the wilderness to meet with them, seeking their wisdom.

As we move through the last days of Advent towards Christmas, why not ponder some of the insights you've gleaned through Zechariah, Elizabeth and John. How might God appear in your life unexpectedly, and, if he does, how will you respond?

Lord Jesus, thank you for coming to earth as a child and for living as one of us. Risen Christ, dwell within me, drawing me closer to you as I serve you with joy and peace.

AMY BOUCHER PYE

The birth and childhood of Jesus

 The Christmas story is probably the best-known part of the Bible, even to those who are not regular churchgoers. But how do people see it? I suspect that for many it is indeed just a story, a 'once upon a time' fable that ranks alongside Snow White and Goldilocks. And to be fair, Christians have colluded: how many Christmas cards have you had depicting the three kings arriving at a somewhat desolate stable? How many nativity plays have starred that overworked and less-than-hospitable innkeeper? How often have you sung about a baby who never cried, even in the bleak midwinter?

Woe, indeed, to the one who presumes to question a much-loved narrative; I will be treading on dangerous ground here! But just how much of this Christmas narrative is fact and how much embroidery? Does the biblical text fully bear the interpretation we bring to it? As with any passage of scripture, there will always be issues of translation – in this case, from the Aramaic spoken by Jesus and his contemporaries into Greek – and of how the material for each gospel was edited. The gospels are indeed factual, historical documents but recorded with a particular theological intent: in Luke's case, to reveal Jesus as the Saviour of the world.

Of course, we are entitled – invited, even – to use our imagination when we read scripture. But we are not to accord to our imaginings the authority of the word of God or write them into every retelling of the story. We can be sure that nothing of value will be lost, and maybe something gained from taking a somewhat critical look at this narrative – that is my hope.

For such an amazing event, the Christmas narrative is remarkably restrained: no purple passages, no detail, no hype. And when we come to the childhood of Jesus, we have even less to go on, apart from apocryphal stories of carved birds being made to fly. But we must surely trust that we have been told all we need to know in order to believe that the Saviour of the world has indeed come among us.

SHEILA WALKER

Grace and favour

In the sixth month the angel Gabriel was sent by God to a town in Galilee called Nazareth, to a virgin engaged to a man whose name was Joseph, of the house of David. The virgin's name was Mary. And he came to her and said, 'Greetings, favoured one! The Lord is with you.' But she was much perplexed by his words and pondered what sort of greeting this might be. The angel said to her, 'Do not be afraid, Mary, for you have found favour with God. And now, you will conceive in your womb and bear a son, and you will name him Jesus. He will be great, and will be called the Son of the Most High, and the Lord God will give to him the throne of his ancestor David. He will reign over the house of Jacob for ever, and of his kingdom there will be no end.'

A grace and favour is a residential property owned by a monarch and leased, often rent-free, to an employee or as thanks for services rendered. Here, however, is the first inkling that the coming Messiah will turn things upside down, for it is the King of kings who seeks the favour of a lodging – in an obscure village in a denigrated part of the country, in a respectable but not highly educated builder's home. Nazareth might have had a couple of hundred residents; Galilee was cosmopolitan rather than 'properly' Jewish; and Joseph was a general builder whose ancestors enjoyed a significant if mixed reputation.

No wonder Mary was 'perplexed' – surely an understatement when confronted with an angel, who then defines the favour of God in a startling and seemingly impossible way.

Our picture of angels will probably owe much to artists' representations, but the New Testament offers little except the occasional reference to 'shining'. They are not always recognised immediately, though they are spoken of in a matter-of-fact way as though their presence, if infrequent, is not unusual. Might we, too, have entertained one without realising it?

Gracious God, your ways are higher than ours, and may often surprise,
even perplex us. May we have the grace to discern your presence in our
lives, in whatever form you choose to take.

SHEILA WALKER

Let it be…

Mary said to the angel, 'How can this be, since I am a virgin?' The angel said to her, 'The Holy Spirit will come upon you, and the power of the Most High will overshadow you; therefore the child to be born will be holy; he will be called Son of God. And now, your relative Elizabeth in her old age has also conceived a son; and this is the sixth month for her who was said to be barren. For nothing will be impossible with God.' Then Mary said, 'Here am I, the servant of the Lord; let it be with me according to your word.' Then the angel departed from her.

The account of Jesus' miraculous conception will tend to polarise opinion between those who hold that anything beyond our normal experience is impossible and those for whom the surprising, even the apparently impossible, can never be beyond a sovereign God.

True, the passage from Isaiah speaks of a 'young woman' (Isaiah 7:14) rather than a 'virgin'; true, neither the gospel writers nor the authors of the epistles make anything of this event in their subsequent writings. We might infer, therefore, that belief in Jesus' miraculous conception is not absolutely vital for salvation. Why, then, would Matthew and Luke, the meticulous historian, have included such a testimony were it not on good evidence?

In choosing Mary, God recognises one of those for whom nothing is impossible; one whose faith is 'childlike' in the positive sense of being trusting, refusing to over-analyse or set oneself up in judgement over the word of God. Understandably, she asks, 'How?', but she is content not to understand the detail, the science of the answer. Gabriel has an answer; that is enough. 'Let it be,' she says, simply.

Did she have any choice? Perhaps not. Gabriel does not ask; rather he tells her what will happen. But there is a great difference between resignation and positive acceptance of the will of God for us.

Sovereign Lord, may we not limit you by the meagreness of our own understanding and experience: expand our minds, fire our imagination, deepen our trust and help us to accept our 'lot' as the place where we will find peace and blessing.

SHEILA WALKER

A shoulder to lean on

In those days Mary set out and went with haste to a Judean town in the hill country, where she entered the house of Zechariah and greeted Elizabeth. When Elizabeth heard Mary's greeting, the child leapt in her womb. And Elizabeth was filled with the Holy Spirit, and exclaimed with a loud cry, 'Blessed are you among women, and blessed is the fruit of your womb. And why has this happened to me, that the mother of my Lord comes to me? For as soon as I heard the sound of your greeting, the child in my womb leapt for joy. And blessed is she who believed that there would be a fulfilment of what was spoken to her by the Lord.'

In response to Gabriel's news that her relative Elizabeth is also miraculously pregnant, Mary makes the journey south to visit her. At once, she has confirmation of her amazing calling, as the Holy Spirit reveals both to Elizabeth and to the unborn John the Baptist that Mary is indeed to be the mother of the long-awaited Messiah. In the light of all that we know will follow, the blessing of God that she then pronounces may not appear to be exactly a passport to happiness, but in the light of eternity, we can understand that blessing is perhaps more about the privilege of being chosen, graced, enabled.

What prompted Mary to make this journey? Maybe the need to seek sanctuary from the inevitable gossip, suspicion and disapproval. Maybe the need for reassurance from someone older and wiser, and with six months' experience of a first pregnancy. Maybe because she sensed that this was a veiled suggestion from Gabriel, a provision from the Lord to support and encourage her through this uniquely awe-inspiring yet challenging time. We can sense the excitement, the wonder, the joy of these two women as the child leaps, Elizabeth shouts out her words of blessing and we can imagine them hugging, laughing and crying with that mix of excitement, trepidation and wonder.

Lord, thank you that, although our own calling may at times be perplexing and difficult, you never ask more of us than you enable us to fulfil. Help us to recognise your provision for us and to rejoice in your goodness.

SHEILA WALKER

Praise re-echoes

And Mary said, 'My soul magnifies the Lord, and my spirit rejoices in God my Saviour, for he has looked with favour on the lowliness of his servant. Surely, from now on all generations will call me blessed, for the Mighty One has done great things for me, and holy is his name.'

Consciously or not, Mary's outpouring of praise echoes Hannah's response to God's gift of her son Samuel. Perhaps this is why it has occasionally been suggested that it is Elizabeth rather than Mary who is speaking here, since both she and Hannah were known to be barren. The evidence, however, points to Mary: many of the themes and phraseology here echo in the Psalms, Isaiah and elsewhere in the Old Testament, suggesting perhaps that she has been chosen, in part at least, for her piety and regard for the word of God.

There is an ambiguity around her words that 'all generations will call me blessed': does it mean that she is to be blessed, that is, worshipped or honoured, or that she has indeed been blessed by God? Interpretations vary, in part according to churchmanship. Certainly we are to respect and honour her for what must have been a uniquely demanding responsibility, and take encouragement and inspiration from the fact that God does indeed choose, use and bless those who may be insignificant in the world's eyes.

It would not seem possible, however, to make an easy equation between blessing and happiness as we usually understand the latter. We know that at times Mary was bewildered by her son's behaviour, even thought he was out of his mind, not to mention sharing in her own unique way the agony of his trial and crucifixion. One might argue that the subsequent experience of his resurrection would have been enough to redeem the use of that word 'blessed' and given her a sense of deep joy, if not exactly happiness. But for us, too, our experience of God's blessing may appear mixed indeed.

Lord, help us to view our experience in the light of eternity and of your steadfast love and faithfulness. May we know ourselves blessed indeed.

SHEILA WALKER

Heights of humility

'His mercy is for those who fear him from generation to generation. He has shown strength with his arm; he has scattered the proud in the thoughts of their hearts. He has brought down the powerful from their thrones, and lifted up the lowly; he has filled the hungry with good things, and sent the rich away empty. He has helped his servant Israel, in remembrance of his mercy, according to the promise he made to our ancestors, to Abraham and to his descendants forever.' And Mary remained with her for about three months and then returned to her home.

With its many echoes of Old Testament praise, it is likely that Mary used words familiar to her, which were later written down and maybe elaborated. As one commentator observed, she was unlikely to have composed it extempore! But she sees in her own situation an echo of the character and working of God throughout the history of her people.

The theme of humility is one that will be taken up by Jesus on many occasions, that those who exalt themselves will be humbled and those who humble themselves will be exalted. Awareness of one's own poverty, inadequacy, need and therefore dependence on God is key to our understanding of the beatitudes. Only when we come to him empty-handed are we able to receive mercy, restoration, spiritual food and everything else that is contained in the promises of God.

There is a challenge here to remember to take a long view. The temptation is to be so caught up in the immediate frustrations of our situation – why doesn't God intervene and answer our prayers? – that we forget we are part of a much bigger story in which the workings of God are not always apparent, but are assuredly bringing about the redemption of all things. Mary and Elizabeth could never have imagined all that the future would hold for their unborn children, but their joy and trust can inspire us.

Loving God, grant us grace to trust you in the face of uncertainty,
to rejoice in the certainty of your love and greater purposes for us
and humbly to seek you for all we need to fulfil our calling.

SHEILA WALKER

A time and a place for everything

In those days a decree went out from Emperor Augustus that all the world should be registered. This was the first registration and was taken while Quirinius was governor of Syria. All went to their own towns to be registered. Joseph also went from the town of Nazareth in Galilee to Judea, to the city of David called Bethlehem, because he was descended from the house and family of David. He went to be registered with Mary, to whom he was engaged and who was expecting a child. While they were there, the time came for her to deliver her child. And she gave birth to her firstborn son and wrapped him in bands of cloth, and laid him in a manger, because there was no place for them in the inn.

Our faith is rooted in history. God intervenes in an unprecedented way, the Word made flesh. Luke locates time and place clearly and succinctly: the only problem being that Quirinius was governor of Syria from AD6, but Jesus was born before Herod's death in 4BC. Possibly Quirinius, in a different capacity, initiated the census which was then completed under his governorship.

The fact that Mary and Joseph travel together implies they are effectively married, though describing her as 'engaged' or 'betrothed' indicates that they have not consummated the marriage.

But the overcrowded inn? The much-maligned innkeeper? Those Christmas cards showing isolated barns with mystified oxen looking on? More likely, given the Jewish reputation for hospitality and the fact that Bethlehem is Joseph's 'home town', is that this owes much to dubious translation. The word for 'inn' also means a guest room. Like a Devon longhouse, this room would be at one end, while at the other end, on a slightly lower level, would be the area where animals were housed. It is probable that, in the event of the guest room being already taken, Joseph and Mary would be welcomed in to share the living area, using the manger from the animals' area as a cradle. Not to welcome a descendant of David in Bethlehem, the city of David, would deeply shame the whole community.

Lord, as we engage with text and translation, help us to discern your truth.

SHEILA WALKER

Breaking news

In that region there were shepherds living in the fields, keeping watch over their flock by night. Then an angel of the Lord stood before them, and the glory of the Lord shone around them, and they were terrified. But the angel said to them, 'Do not be afraid; for see – I am bringing you good news of great joy for all the people: to you is born this day in the city of David a Saviour, who is the Messiah, the Lord. This will be a sign for you: you will find a child wrapped in bands of cloth and lying in a manger.' And suddenly there was with the angel a multitude of the heavenly host, praising God and saying, 'Glory to God in the highest heaven, and on earth peace among those whom he favours!'

The circumstances of the birth may have been shockingly, arrestingly humble, but heaven cannot contain its excitement, overflowing in skies (and fields?) filled with angels, the glory of God and an unusual star. The most significant news of all time is announced with the greatest of all massed choirs, not to the religiously or politically important but to the most insignificant of people, whose care, faithfulness and obedience seemingly count for more than the power-seeking self-righteousness of leaders. The lamb of God is revealed first to those who care for lambs: to humble shepherds. While they may not understand it all (who does?), their minds and hearts are open and receptive, enough to respond in wonder and worship.

Again, we see the reversal of values that is to characterise the life and teaching of Jesus: the humble will be exalted, the self-important brought low; and those who are watchful, ever on the alert, may find themselves unexpectedly blessed. It is all too easy to expect God to speak to us in certain ways – through respected speakers, beautiful scenery, places of worship. But in that regard, truly he is no respecter of place or person.

Lord of glory, it is beyond our imagining that you could be fully present in a box of hay. Help us to discern your presence, in whatever manifestation, and to hear your voice, through whatever messenger.

SHEILA WALKER

Telling the story

When the angels had left them and gone into heaven, the shepherds said to one another, 'Let us go now to Bethlehem and see this thing that has taken place, which the Lord has made known to us.' So they went with haste and found Mary and Joseph, and the child lying in the manger. When they saw this, they made known what had been told them about this child; and all who heard it were amazed at what the shepherds told them. But Mary treasured all these words and pondered them in her heart. The shepherds returned, glorifying and praising God for all they had heard and seen, as it had been told them. After eight days had passed, it was time to circumcise the child; and he was called Jesus, the name given by the angel before he was conceived in the womb.

Gabriel has already told Mary that her child will be the 'Son of the Most High', 'Son of God' and ruler over Israel forever and that, conceived by the Holy Spirit, he will be holy. As if all that were not enough even to begin to grasp, the shepherds now add to those prophetic words: he is Saviour, Messiah, Lord – despite the fact that they will find him in the most unlikely place imaginable. Given that the most learned religious leaders will have their ideas of messiah overturned, what a challenge for Mary to hold on to these words in the face of all that will follow.

We can imagine the shepherds pouring out their story to the household gathered around the manger – such extraordinary events, such an extraordinary message! But an example, too, for us – to be open to hear from God, to act on what we believe we hear and then to *tell the story*. We are all called to be witnesses.

Luke tells us that Mary 'treasured' the shepherds' words and 'pondered' them. This, too, is an example – to approach the word of God, written or spoken, with reverence and a willingness to take time to meditate and allow it to work deeply in us, like yeast raising us to new levels of faith, hope and love.

Lord, enable us not keep your word to ourselves but tell it like it is.

SHEILA WALKER

Law-abiding

When the time came for their purification according to the law of Moses, they brought him up to Jerusalem to present him to the Lord (as it is written in the law of the Lord, 'Every firstborn male shall be designated as holy to the Lord'), and they offered a sacrifice according to what is stated in the law of the Lord, 'a pair of turtle-doves or two young pigeons'. Now there was a man in Jerusalem whose name was Simeon; this man was righteous and devout, looking forward to the consolation of Israel, and the Holy Spirit rested on him.

Under the law of Moses, after the birth of a male child, his mother is regarded as unclean for seven days and has to remain at home for a further 33 days; then a purification sacrifice must be offered. A firstborn child has to be redeemed – an animal is sacrificed, but a human child is redeemed by paying five shekels when they are a month old. The child does not need to be present, but it seems that Mary wants specially to dedicate her child to God, just as Hannah offered Samuel.

What stands out in this passage is Mary and Joseph's scrupulous observance of the requirements of the law, echoed in the description of Simeon as 'righteous and devout': that is, in right relationship with God and wholehearted in his practice of worship. Although we are told that the Holy Spirit rests on him, this is not yet the age of the new covenant, when the Holy Spirit is poured out and salvation comes by faith, rather than by works. For now, all are living still under the old covenant, under law, though grace is just around the corner. Faithfulness, then, is marked by attention to what is required by 'the law of the Lord' and a steadfast trust that his promises will be fulfilled, however long that may take.

And that is surely all that is asked of any of us: to walk faithfully in whatever light we have received.

God of revelation, may we be wholehearted in our response to all you have already shown us, and to hunger and thirst for more of your righteousness, truth and love.

SHEILA WALKER

Mixed blessing

Guided by the Spirit, Simeon came into the temple; and when the parents brought in the child Jesus, to do for him what was customary under the law, Simeon took him in his arms and praised God, saying, 'Master, now you are dismissing your servant in peace, according to your word; for my eyes have seen your salvation, which you have prepared in the presence of all peoples, a light for revelation to the Gentiles and for glory to your people Israel.' And the child's father and mother were amazed at what was being said about him. Then Simeon blessed them and said to his mother Mary, 'This child is destined for the falling and the rising of many in Israel, and to be a sign that will be opposed so that the inner thoughts of many will be revealed – and a sword will pierce your own soul too.'

This beautiful cameo portrait of Simeon is one of the jewels of this narrative of Jesus' early years. We see him as a man wholly committed to God, all his senses tuned to that divine wavelength. First, he *hears* from God the promise that he will not die until he has seen the Messiah. Second, he *sees*: he recognises that this particular child is the uniquely special one. Third, he *acts*: he engages with the family, taking the child in his arms. Fourth, he *speaks*, boldly declaring the words God has given him, amazing and difficult though they must have been to receive. This is surely a compelling example of what it means to be a true servant of the Lord.

For Simeon, it means that he can now depart this life with a sense of satisfaction, knowing that there are no loose ends, that all that God has planned for him is completed. At one time, the whole purpose of education was thought to be so that we could 'make a good death'; perhaps the fact that Anglicans continue to use Simeon's prayer, the Nunc Dimittis, reflects this unspoken desire.

Gracious God, may we be tuned in to all that you plan for us
and respond with faithfulness and courage, humility and love.

SHEILA WALKER

Confirmation

There was also a prophet, Anna, the daughter of Phanuel, of the tribe of Asher. She was of a great age, having lived with her husband for seven years after her marriage, then as a widow to the age of eighty-four. She never left the temple but worshipped there with fasting and prayer night and day. At that moment she came, and began to praise God and to speak about the child to all who were looking for the redemption of Jerusalem. When they had finished everything required by the law of the Lord, they returned to Galilee, to their own town of Nazareth. The child grew and became strong, filled with wisdom; and the favour of God was upon him.

Luke is famous for the attention he gives to those who are often marginalised. He includes details of Jesus' childhood, and here he highlights the witness of a woman. Anna confirms Simeon's insight, not only to Mary and Joseph here in the temple but presumably in the days that followed to others who are faithfully awaiting the Messiah. She is not the first or the last woman in the Bible with the gift of prophecy – we might remember Deborah or Philip's four daughters; women's ministry has a long history!

Anna's dedication – even if she does not literally spend every moment in the temple – is impressive. And what joy she must have experienced towards the close of a long life, to be rewarded with this encounter with her Messiah.

Anna is blessed with the knowledge that her lifetime of prayer and prophecy is even now being fulfilled. That has not always been the case, nor will it be for us. The call will often be to persevere in faith, knowing only that God has entrusted us with that desire to reach out to him, trusting the time and outworking to him. We are to walk more by faith, less by sight, faith being the substance of things hoped for but not yet seen.

Lord, we ask that you will move us to deeper levels of prayer,
together with the grace to persevere.

SHEILA WALKER

A most promising pupil

Now every year his parents went to Jerusalem for the festival of the Passover. And when he was twelve years old, they went up as usual for the festival. When the festival was ended and they started to return, the boy Jesus stayed behind in Jerusalem, but his parents did not know it. Assuming that he was in the group of travellers, they went a day's journey. Then they started to look for him among their relatives and friends. When they did not find him, they returned to Jerusalem to search for him. After three days they found him in the temple, sitting among the teachers, listening to them and asking them questions. And all who heard him were amazed at his understanding and his answers.

At the age of twelve a boy is prepared to enter the religious community as an adult and, at Passover time, whole families travel to Jerusalem, swelling its population from around 25,000 to up to 100,000. Little wonder, then, that on that first day's journey home, Mary and Joseph do not miss Jesus among the crowd of friends and relatives, especially as there are younger siblings to look after. Luke tells it in a matter-of-fact way, but we can imagine their anxiety and frustration at having to travel back and search among the crowds; is the temple the first or last place they think to look?

This is the only glimpse we have of Jesus as a boy, but here we see already the work of the Holy Spirit, preparing him for what lies ahead. Often people speculate as to how much Jesus understood of God's calling. It seems that, as it is for us, it was a step-by-step revelation as he responds to the promptings of the Spirit. Evidently he feels drawn to those who can explain those scriptures which, uniquely, he is to fulfil, and they recognise in him a depth of understanding that astonishes them in one so young. There is no indication, however, that any of them as yet either know or recall the words of Simeon and Anna and therefore suspect that here, indeed, is their Messiah.

Lord, help us to recognise and encourage your work
in the lives of our children and young people.

SHEILA WALKER

Father

When his parents saw him they were astonished; and his mother said to him, 'Child, why have you treated us like this? Look, your father and I have been searching for you in great anxiety.' He said to them, 'Why were you searching for me? Did you not know that I must be in my Father's house?' But they did not understand what he said to them. Then he went down with them and came to Nazareth, and was obedient to them. His mother treasured all these things in her heart. And Jesus increased in wisdom and in years, and in divine and human favour.

We have heard about Jesus, and something of his future ministry, from both angels and prophets; now, for the first time, we hear from Jesus himself. Although the Jews always spoke of God as being, in some way, their Father, this is probably along the lines of him being the one who brought the nation of Israel into being. Jesus' words here indicate a much more intimate, personal sense of the fatherhood of God. And this will constitute a key element of his mission: to bring others into a similar relationship, as children of God, born again through the Holy Spirit, signed through the water of baptism.

Any parent will know how easy it is to have a failure of emotional intelligence when it comes to understanding their child – or vice versa: what is obvious to one is a complete mystery to the other. Here, Jesus probably intends no disrespect; he is simply where his Father would want him to be. Hard, though, for Joseph, in the ever-challenging role of stepparent, to realise that his fathering of Jesus, however good, can never hold a candle to the unique kinship he has with his heavenly Father.

One of the challenges of the story of Jesus' early years is that we move so quickly: here, 30 years in less than two chapters. We know only that Jesus is seen to be wise and well thought of by all. It won't last.

Heavenly Father, whatever our situation, help us to know ourselves ever more fully as your children, thanks to your Son, our Lord Jesus Christ.

SHEILA WALKER

Introducing BRF's advocates lead

Jane Butcher has been BRF's advocates lead since September 2020. Jane is no stranger to BRF, having joined the team 13 years ago working with Barnabas in Schools and our Children and Families ministry.

As BRF seeks to further develop and celebrate volunteering across the organisation, one of Jane's key roles is to work with our volunteer managers to ensure all our volunteers have a rewarding and enjoyable experience with BRF. She also hopes to encourage more people to join us by raising awareness of our volunteer opportunities.

Jane is also gathering a team of volunteer advocates to share the work of BRF – our ministries, resources and support offering – in their local church and surrounding area.

Could you help or do you know someone who could?

Whether you have a little or a lot of time, previous experience of advocating or none, we would love to hear from you! We are looking for people of all ages who have a heart for what BRF does to help us raise awareness of our work and invite even more people to be a part of it.

All BRF volunteers can be assured of a warm welcome, ongoing support and appreciation as a valued part of our team.

If you or anyone you know might be interested in becoming an advocate for BRF, please email Jane at **jane.butcher@brf.org.uk**.

Become a Friend of BRF
and give regularly
to support our ministry

We help people of all ages to grow in faith

We encourage and support individual Christians and churches as they serve and resource the changing spiritual needs of communities today.

Through Anna Chaplaincy
we're enabling churches to provide spiritual care to older people

Through Living Faith
we're nurturing faith and resourcing life-long discipleship

Through Messy Church
we're helping churches to reach out to families

Through Parenting for Faith
we're supporting parents as they raise their children in the Christian faith

Our ministry is only possible because of the generous support of individuals, churches, trusts and gifts in wills.

As we look to the future and make plans, **regular donations make a huge difference** in ensuring we can both start and finish projects well.

By becoming a Friend of BRF and giving regularly to our ministry you are partnering with us in the gospel and helping change lives.

How your gift makes a difference

£2 a month — Helps us to develop **Living Faith** resources to use in care homes and communities

£10 a month — Helps us to support churches running the **Parenting for Faith** course and stand alongside parents

£5 a month — Helps us to support **Messy Church** volunteers and resource and grow the wider network

£20 a month — Helps us to resource **Anna Chaplaincy** and improve spiritual care for older people

 ## How to become a Friend of BRF

Set up a Direct Debit donation at **brf.org.uk/donate** or find out how to set up a Standing Order at **brf.org.uk/friends**

Contact the fundraising team

Email: **giving@brf.org.uk**
Tel: +44 (0)1235 462305
Post: Fundraising team, BRF, 15 The Chambers, Vineyard, Abingdon OX14 3FE

Good to know

If you have any questions, or if you want to change your regular donation or stop giving in the future, do get in touch.

Registered with

FUNDRAISING **REGULATOR**

SHARING OUR VISION – MAKING A ONE-OFF GIFT

I would like to make a donation to support BRF.
Please use my gift for:

☐ Where it is most needed ☐ Anna Chaplaincy ☐ Living Faith
☐ Messy Church ☐ Parenting for Faith

Title	First name/initials	Surname
Address		
		Postcode
Email		
Telephone		
Signature		Date

Our ministry is only possible because of the generous support of individuals, churches, trusts and gifts in wills.

gift aid it   You can add an extra 25p to every £1 you give.

Please treat as Gift Aid donations all qualifying gifts of money made

☐ today, ☐ in the past four years, ☐ and in the future.

I am a UK taxpayer and understand that if I pay less Income Tax and/or Capital Gains Tax in the current tax year than the amount of Gift Aid claimed on all my donations, it is my responsibility to pay any difference.

☐ My donation does not qualify for Gift Aid.

Please notify BRF if you want to cancel this Gift Aid declaration, change your name or home address, or no longer pay sufficient tax on your income and/or capital gains.

Please complete other side of form ➲

SHARING OUR VISION – MAKING A ONE-OFF GIFT

Please accept my gift of:

☐ £2 ☐ £5 ☐ £10 ☐ £20 Other £ ☐

by (*delete as appropriate*):

☐ Cheque/Charity Voucher payable to 'BRF'

☐ MasterCard/Visa/Debit card/Charity card

Name on card

Card no. ☐☐☐☐ ☐☐☐☐ ☐☐☐☐ ☐☐☐☐

Expires end ☐☐ ☐☐ (M M Y Y) Security code* ☐☐☐

*Last 3 digits on the reverse of the card
ESSENTIAL IN ORDER TO PROCESS
YOUR PAYMENT

Signature   Date

☐ I would like to leave a gift to BRF in my will.
   Please send me further information.

For help or advice regarding making a gift, please contact
our fundraising team +44 (0)1865 462305

Your privacy

We will use your personal data to process this transaction.
From time to time we may send you information about
the work of BRF that we think may be of interest to you.
Our privacy policy is available at **brf.org.uk/privacy**.
Please contact us if you wish to discuss your mailing
preferences.

Registered with

FR

FUNDRAISING
REGULATOR

← Please complete other side of form

Please return this form to 'Freepost BRF'
No other address information or stamp is needed

The Bible Reading Fellowship is a Registered Charity (233280)

Reading *New Daylight* in a group

SALLY WELCH

I am aware that although some of you cherish the moments of quiet during the day which enable you to read and reflect on the passages we offer you in *New Daylight,* other readers prefer to study in small groups, to enable conversation and discussion and the sharing of insights. With this in mind, here are some ideas for discussion starters within a study group. Some of the questions are generic and can be applied to any set of contributions within this issue; others are specific to certain sets of readings. I hope they generate some interesting reflections and conversations!

General discussion starters

These can be used for any study series within this issue. Remember there are no right or wrong answers – these questions are simply to enable a group to engage in conversation.

- What do you think the main idea or theme of the author in this series? Do you think they succeeded in communicating this to you, or were you more interested in the side issues?

- Have you had any experience of the issues that are raised in the study? How have they affected your life?

- What evidence does the author use to support their ideas? Do they use personal observations and experience, facts, quotations from other authorities? Which appeals to you most?

- Does the author make a 'call to action'? Is that call realistic and achievable? Do you think their ideas will work in the secular world?

- Can you identify specific passages that struck you personally – as interesting, profound, difficult to understand or illuminating?

- Did you learn something new reading this series? Will you think differently about some things, and if so, what are they?

Questions for specific series
Eating together (Lakshmi Jeffreys)
Lakshmi reflects on the notion of 'feeding our enemies'. What do you think can be gained by doing this? In what ways might this happen?
   Which is easier – offering or accepting hospitality?

'I was hungry and you gave me food' (Matthew 25:35, NRSV). How do you feed the hungry? How does your church do this? Are there ways in which you could do more?

The four last things: hell (Murdo Macdonald)

Murdo Macdonald asks us in his introduction, 'If we go to the recorded words of Jesus, is it honest or balanced to accept his statements about heaven, while choosing to ignore or reject those concerning hell?' (p. 94). What do you think?

Murdo quotes Rob Bell saying, 'A good sermon is going to disturb the comfortable and comfort the disturbed. It inspires you. It provokes you. It should make your soul soar' (p. 94). What makes a good sermon?

Zechariah (Amy Boucher Pye)

'God may choose to visit us through an angel… or through less dramatic means, such as his Holy Spirit highlighting a passage of the Bible for us' (p. 113). Have you experienced a visitation from God? What was it like? What was the result for you?

Zechariah reflects God's glory in an indirect way – he is father to John, who points towards Christ. Can you think of ways in which you have reflected God's glory, directly or indirectly?

Isaiah (Sally Welch)

The word that Isaiah son of Amoz saw concerning Judah and Jerusalem. In days to come the mountain of the Lord's house shall be established as the highest of the mountains, and shall be raised above the hills; all the nations shall stream to it.

ISAIAH 2:1 (NRSV)

Isaiah calls us to 'walk in the light of the Lord'. What does that expression mean for you? How might we all walk in the light of the Lord? What is your vision for the future of the world's people?

Meet the author: Stephen Rand

I began my working life as a history teacher – having been a revolting student (it was the end of the '60s) and struggling to hold on to my faith inside a church that seemed unmoved by famine, poverty and injustice.

So discovering Tearfund was significant – Christians concerned enough to do something about these things. Susan and I were just married, first baby, struggling to make ends meet – what could we do to help make a difference? We became Tearcraft reps, which allowed me to play at shop-keeping while trying to change the world, one Bangladesh jute handicraft at a time.

Setting up Tearcraft stalls in church halls (once in the Albert Hall) became our main spare-time activity. Then I discovered Tearfund were advertising for someone to develop their volunteer network, and to my amazement I found myself privileged to be paid to do what I cared about most.

I worked at Tearfund for 25 years, and I was thrilled to establish advocacy – campaigning for change – there. When I left, I found myself doing the same thing at Open Doors. It was making contact with parliamentarians on behalf of Christians facing persecution that led to my involvement with the All-Party Parliamentary Group for International Freedom of Religion or Belief. When I retired from full-time work with Open Doors, I offered to look after their website and make sure that MPs and peers in the group were kept informed about people facing persecution because of their faith, so they can use their influence to bring about change. And some do!

Over the years, I have been variously involved in Christian leadership, both nationally and in local Baptist churches. Recently, I've just become a member of our church leadership team – they assured me I wasn't too old! It's great to see people growing and developing in faith, and I've been particularly active in encouraging the church to meet the challenge of the new housing estates in Bicester, reputedly the fastest growing town in Europe.

And, joy of joys, just as our first two grandchildren were reaching the age when Grandad probably is too old, our younger daughter blessed us with Stella, who still gets excited at seeing Grandma and Grandad – and helps me remember just how old I am!

Recommended reading

Advent is a time to remember and reflect on the Christmas story and the baby at its heart. But the virgin birth, the manger, the mysterious eastern visitors and their portentous gifts – all these hint at a much grander narrative. Come and explore the whole Christmas story, and find your place within it.

The following is an edited extract from the introduction to *The Whole Christmas Story*, by Jo Swinney.

When we talk about the Christmas story, we are generally covering the ground between the angel Gabriel's visit to Mary and Joseph, Mary and Jesus' escape to Egypt. These events are recounted in the gospels of Matthew and Luke: 120 verses between them. The details are few and familiar. A young virgin suddenly pregnant, her fiancé shamed. A reassuring dream for Joseph and a soothing visit to an older relative for Mary. A journey to a far-off town for a census, the discovery that all guest rooms are full and the newborn Jesus laid in a manger. A visit from some shepherds and the Magi, whose arrival alerts King Herod to a pretender to his throne.

Understandably, at this time of year we think a great deal about this story. You might imagine a book created to help you engage with the season on a spiritual level would take you through the relevant sections of Matthew and Luke, perhaps coming at them at a new angle or showing them in a different light. There are many wonderful Advent devotionals that do this. I have used them and found them helpful.

But I want to do something different here. I want us to think about how Christmas sits in the whole Christian story, from Genesis to Revelation. I want to take us up a steep and winding path to a high vantage point, from where we can survey the horizon in all directions. Or, to use a more specifically 21st-century metaphor, let's play with Google Earth, starting in outer space and zooming in further and further until we are sitting, mesmerised and worshipful by a makeshift cradle and the God-baby inside it. Who is Jesus, and what is his cosmic significance? Who was he to the generations who came and went before his birth, and who is he to those of us living long after? Why did God take on human form, and what do we do with all those not completely fulfilled promises of healing and deliverance?

Please don't expect tidy answers to those huge questions in these pages. They aren't there. But the Bible does take us into the heart of God's purposes for his creation and if we come humbly and open to the task, he will open our eyes as we read and explore over this Advent season.

On a personal note, I have to confess that, over the years, hearing the Christmas story told in a secular context has sometimes made me cringe a bit inside. It all seemed so far-fetched when given an airing among purportedly rational, educated and sophisticated people: a quaint and primitive fairy story for those willing to suspend disbelief in the name of faith. I wondered if in my heart of hearts, I actually believed it. I suspected it would take a real test to show me my true mettle as a self-professed Jesus follower.

I started work on this book in September 2019. On 28 October, just under two months later, I spent the morning writing. I was on track to hand in a completed manuscript by my January deadline and my mum, who has worked with me on all my books, was in the wings to go through an early draft as soon as I had one to give her.

After lunch, I did a superficial house tidy and packed for a few days away. Around 3.30 pm, I set off with my husband, Shawn, and our daughters, Alexa and Charis, for a half-term break in a remote cottage we had rented. My husband Shawn's phone rang five minutes into our journey, as we were driving down a steep road outside Bath called Brassknocker Hill. It was my uncle Steve, and he asked Shawn to pull over and give him a call back.

Once they had spoken, Shawn got back in the car with red eyes and said we had to go back home. Something really bad had happened, and he'd tell us what it was when we had got into the house. Both girls started crying and asking questions. I told them whatever the news was, God was good, and he loved us, and we'd be okay.

The news was life-altering. My parents had been in a terrible car accident in South Africa, where they had been on a work trip with the charity they had founded, A Rocha. My mother had been killed along with two colleagues and friends, Chris and Susanna Naylor. The driver was alive, and my father was in critical condition. I'm so glad I can tell you he miraculously survived with no long-term physical injuries.

Subsequent weeks and months have been painful and dark. Grief hits me like a kind of reverse labour, with contractions coming further apart with time. The intensity of loss can take my breath away, but it recedes and somehow life goes on.

Even at the beginning, when there was barely a second's reprieve from howling hurt and shock, I had no questions for God. I realised my belief that he was real, he was good and he was loving went deep. I sensed the Holy Spirit brooding over the troubled waters of my distress. Silent, yes, but present, working redemption even as I thrashed around, fearing I'd drown.

My mum loved Christmas. She would start playing wall to wall carols on 1 December (we'd banned her from starting earlier), bake dozens of mince pies and spend hours lovingly wrapping the gifts she'd been stockpiling all year. Our Christmas tree was always the best tree of all the trees, and she'd often sit in the glow of its lights late in the evening in child-like delight.

We did our best to celebrate our first Christmas without her, telling ourselves she'd have wanted us to give the grandchildren a happy day. Without her, our clan numbers 17, and we were all together. I'm not sure we celebrated, but we managed to get through it. Christmas without her is never going to be the same.

One thing I know: the Christmas baby has given me a sure and certain hope that one day I will see her again and we will be together in the unveiled presence of the triune God. As Zechariah said after the birth of his own miraculous son, John, Jesus has given us 'salvation through the forgiveness of [our] sins, because of the tender mercy of our God, by which the rising sun will come to us from heaven to shine on those living in darkness and in the shadow of death' (Luke 1:77–79). This is the big picture. This is the context. This is how the whole thing makes sense.

To order a copy of this book, please use the order form on page 151 or visit **brfonline.org.uk**

Enjoy a little luxury: upgrade to *New Daylight deluxe*

Many readers enjoy the compact format of the regular *New Daylight* but more and more people are discovering the advantages of the larger format, premium edition, *New Daylight deluxe*. The pocket-sized version is perfect if you're reading on the move but the larger print, white paper and extra space to write your own notes and comments all make the deluxe edition an attractive alternative and significant upgrade.

Why not try it to see if you like it? You can order single copies at brfonline.org.uk/newdaylightdeluxe

Deluxe actual size:

gladness instead of mourning, the mantle of spirit. They will be called oaks of righteousness to display his glory.

We learn from these verses that gladness is first them' gladness instead of mourning and praise i gift needs to be received, and action is often re gift. For example, receiving a piano is of little u play it. God has blessed us with 'every spiritual but, metaphorically speaking, *we* have to pour o put on and wear the mantle of praise. The Lord

To order

Online: brfonline.org.uk
Telephone: +44 (0)1865 319700
Mon–Fri 9.30–17.00

Delivery times within the UK are normally 15 working days. Prices are correct at the time of going to press but may change without prior notice.

Title	Price	Qty	Total
The BRF Book of 365 Bible Reflections	£14.99		
Celebrating Christmas	£8.99		
The Whole Christmas Story	£8.99		

POSTAGE AND PACKING CHARGES			
Order value	UK	Europe	Rest of world
Under £7.00	£2.00		
£7.00–£29.99	£3.00	Available on request	Available on request
£30.00 and over	FREE		

Total value of books	
Postage and packing	
Donation*	
Total for this order	

* Please complete and return the Gift Aid declaration on page 141.

Please complete in BLOCK CAPITALS

Title .... First name/initials .... Surname ....

Address ....

.... Postcode ....

Acc. No. .... Telephone ....

Email ....

Method of payment

❏ Cheque (made payable to BRF) ❏ MasterCard / Visa

Card no. ☐☐☐☐ ☐☐☐☐ ☐☐☐☐ ☐☐☐☐

Expires end ☐☐ ☐☐   Security code* ☐☐☐   Last 3 digits on the reverse of the card

Signature* .... Date .... / .... / ....

*ESSENTIAL IN ORDER TO PROCESS YOUR ORDER

Please return this form to:
BRF, 15 The Chambers, Vineyard, Abingdon OX14 3FE | **enquiries@brf.org.uk**
To read our terms and find out about cancelling your order, please visit **brfonline.org.uk/terms**.

The Bible Reading Fellowship (BRF) is a Registered Charity (233280)

BRF needs you!

If you're one of our many thousands of regular *New Daylight* readers, you will know all about the rich rewards of regular Bible reading and the value of daily notes to guide, inform and inspire you.

Here are some recent comments from *New Daylight* readers:

'Thank you for all the many inspiring writings that help so much when things are tough.'

'Just right for me – I learned a lot!'

'We looked forward to each day's message as we pondered each passage and comment.'

If you have similarly positive things to say about *New Daylight*, would you be willing to help spread the word about these popular resources? Could you follow the example of long-standing *New Daylight* reader Beryl Fudge and form a *New Daylight* reading group, not to take the place of private prayer and reading but to share insights and deepen understanding? 'I've quite a few friends who also take the notes and we discuss them in the group,' says Beryl. 'There's so much in them every day. What I most value in *New Daylight* is the way they connect the Old and New Testament scriptures with what's happening here and now.'

It doesn't need to be complicated: every issue of *New Daylight* includes questions for reflection or discussion.

We can supply further information if you need it and would love to hear about it if you do form a *New Daylight* reading group.

For more information:

- Email **enquiries@brf.org.uk**
- Telephone BRF on +44 (0)1865 319700 Mon–Fri 9.30–17.00
- Write to us at BRF, 15 The Chambers, Vineyard, Abingdon OX14 3FE

Enabling all ages to grow in faith

At BRF, we long for people of all ages to grow in faith and understanding of the Bible. That's what all our work as a charity is about.

- Our **Living Faith** range of resources helps Christians go deeper in their understanding of scripture, in prayer and in their walk with God. Our conferences and events bring people together to share this journey, while our Holy Habits resources help whole congregations grow together as disciples of Jesus, living out and sharing their faith.

- We also want to make it easier for local churches to engage effectively in ministry and mission – by helping them bring new families into a growing relationship with God through **Messy Church** or by supporting churches as they nurture the spiritual life of older people through **Anna Chaplaincy**.

- Our **Parenting for Faith** team coaches parents and others to raise God-connected children and teens, and enables churches to fully support them.

Do you share our vision?

Though a significant proportion of BRF's funding is generated through our charitable activities, we are dependent on the generous support of individuals, churches and charitable trusts.

If you share our vision, would you help us to enable even more people of all ages to grow in faith? Your prayers and financial support are vital for the work that we do. You could:

- Support BRF's ministry with a regular donation;
- Support us with a one-off gift;
- Consider leaving a gift to BRF in your will (see page 154);
- Encourage your church to support BRF as part of your church's giving to home mission – perhaps focusing on a specific ministry or programme;
- Most important of all, support BRF with your prayers.

Donate at **brf.org.uk/donate** or use the form on pages 141–42.

Speaking and sharing good news with vulnerable, yet valued, members of society

There was also a prophet, Anna, the daughter of Penuel, of the tribe of Asher. She was very old… She never left the temple but worshipped night and day, fasting and praying. Coming up to them at that very moment, she gave thanks to God and spoke about the child to all who were looking forward to the redemption of Jerusalem.

LUKE 2:36–38 (NIV, abridged)

Anna Chaplaincy
for older people

When Jesus was brought to the temple and after Simon uttered his famous prayer, Anna steps into the limelight and prophesies of the redemption of Jerusalem. It is from Anna that BRF's ministry – Anna Chaplaincy for Older People – draws its name. Anna spoke of redemption, hope and God's good plan.

It is this same hope that more than 150 Anna Chaplains seek to share with older people across the country. While the pandemic hindered face-to-face ministry, God found a way. One Anna Chaplain, Elizabeth, conducted mini services with one person after another by phone. She read a Bible passage, sang hymns and offered prayers and thanksgivings. Many others found ways to continue ministering at this trying time.

Anna Chaplains help older people in care remain connected to other people and to those aspects of life which bring meaning and purpose to them.

Sustaining and growing this ministry is only possible because of generous donations from donors, churches, charitable trusts and gifts in wills. You can find out more at **brf.org.uk/annachaplaincy**. Please consider whether you or your church could support this ministry financially. You can get in touch with the fundraising team via **giving@brf.org.uk**, on 01235 462305 or by post.

Your prayers, as ever, are hugely appreciated.

Pray. Give. Get involved.
brf.org.uk

Please note our new subscription rates, current until 30 April 2022:

Individual subscriptions
covering 3 issues for under 5 copies, payable in advance
(including postage & packing):

	UK	Europe	Rest of world
New Daylight	£18.00	£25.95	£29.85
New Daylight 3-year subscription (9 issues) (not available for Deluxe)	£52.65	N/A	N/A
New Daylight Deluxe per set of 3 issues p.a.	£22.35	£32.55	£38.55

Group subscriptions
covering 3 issues for 5 copies or more, sent to one UK address (post free):

New Daylight	£14.25 per set of 3 issues p.a.
New Daylight Deluxe	£17.85 per set of 3 issues p.a.

Please note that the annual billing period for group subscriptions runs from 1 May to 30 April.

Overseas group subscription rates
Available on request. Please email **enquiries@brf.org.uk**.

Copies may also be obtained from Christian bookshops:

New Daylight	£4.75 per copy
New Daylight Deluxe	£5.95 per copy

All our Bible reading notes can be ordered online by visiting
brfonline.org.uk/subscriptions

New Daylight is also available as an app for
Android, iPhone and iPad
brfonline.org.uk/apps

NEW DAYLIGHT INDIVIDUAL SUBSCRIPTION FORM

All our Bible reading notes can be ordered online by visiting
brfonline.org.uk/subscriptions

☐ I would like to take out a subscription:

Title .... First name/initials .... Surname ....
Address ....
.... Postcode ....
Telephone .... Email ....

Please send *New Daylight* beginning with the January 2022 / May 2022 /
September 2022 issue (*delete as appropriate*):

(*please tick box*)	UK	Europe	Rest of world
New Daylight 1-year subscription	☐ £18.00	☐ £25.95	☐ £29.85
New Daylight 3-year subscription	☐ £52.65	N/A	N/A
New Daylight Deluxe	☐ £22.35	☐ £32.55	☐ £38.55

Optional donation to support the work of BRF £ ....

Total enclosed £ .... (cheques should be made payable to 'BRF')

Please complete and return the Gift Aid declaration on page 141 to make your
donation even more valuable to us.

Please charge my MasterCard / Visa ☐ Debit card ☐ with £ ....

Card no. ☐☐☐☐ ☐☐☐☐ ☐☐☐☐ ☐☐☐☐

Expires end ☐☐ ☐☐ Security code* ☐☐☐ Last 3 digits on the reverse of the card

Signature* .... Date .... /....... /.......

*ESSENTIAL IN ORDER TO PROCESS YOUR PAYMENT

To set up a Direct Debit, please also complete the Direct Debit instruction on page 159
and return it to BRF with this form.

Please return this form with the appropriate payment to:
BRF, 15 The Chambers, Vineyard, Abingdon OX14 3FE

To read our terms and find out about cancelling your order,
please visit **brfonline.org.uk/terms**.

ND0321

NEW DAYLIGHT GIFT SUBSCRIPTION FORM

☐ I would like to give a gift subscription (please provide both names and addresses):

Title _____ First name/initials _____ Surname _____

Address _____

_____ Postcode _____

Telephone _____ Email _____

Gift subscription name _____

Gift subscription address _____

_____ Postcode _____

Gift message (20 words max. or include your own gift card):

_____

_____

Please send *New Daylight* beginning with the January 2022 / May 2022 / September 2022 issue (*delete as appropriate*):

(*please tick box*)	UK	Europe	Rest of world
New Daylight 1-year subscription	☐ £18.00	☐ £25.95	☐ £29.85
New Daylight 3-year subscription	☐ £52.65	N/A	N/A
New Daylight Deluxe	☐ £22.35	☐ £32.55	☐ £38.55

Optional donation to support the work of BRF £ _____

Total enclosed £ _____ (cheques should be made payable to 'BRF')

Please complete and return the Gift Aid declaration on page 141 to make your donation even more valuable to us.

Please charge my MasterCard / Visa ☐ Debit card ☐ with £ _____

Card no. ☐☐☐☐ ☐☐☐☐ ☐☐☐☐ ☐☐☐☐

Expires end ☐☐☐☐ Security code* ☐☐☐ Last 3 digits on the reverse of the card

Signature* _____ Date _____ /_____ /_____

*ESSENTIAL IN ORDER TO PROCESS YOUR PAYMENT

To set up a Direct Debit, please also complete the Direct Debit instruction on page 159 and return it to BRF with this form.

Please return this form with the appropriate payment to:
BRF, 15 The Chambers, Vineyard, Abingdon OX14 3FE

To read our terms and find out about cancelling your order, please visit **brfonline.org.uk/terms**.

The Bible Reading Fellowship is a Registered Charity (233280)

DIRECT DEBIT PAYMENT

You can pay for your annual subscription to our Bible reading notes using Direct Debit. You need only give your bank details once, and the payment is made automatically every year until you cancel it. If you would like to pay by Direct Debit, please use the form opposite, entering your BRF account number under 'Reference number'.

You are fully covered by the Direct Debit Guarantee:

The Direct Debit Guarantee

- This Guarantee is offered by all banks and building societies that accept instructions to pay Direct Debits.

- If there are any changes to the amount, date or frequency of your Direct Debit, The Bible Reading Fellowship will notify you 10 working days in advance of your account being debited or as otherwise agreed. If you request The Bible Reading Fellowship to collect a payment, confirmation of the amount and date will be given to you at the time of the request.

- If an error is made in the payment of your Direct Debit, by The Bible Reading Fellowship or your bank or building society, you are entitled to a full and immediate refund of the amount paid from your bank or building society.

- If you receive a refund you are not entitled to, you must pay it back when The Bible Reading Fellowship asks you to.

- You can cancel a Direct Debit at any time by simply contacting your bank or building society. Written confirmation may be required. Please also notify us.

The Bible Reading Fellowship

Instruction to your bank or building society to pay by Direct Debit

Please fill in the whole form using a ballpoint pen and return it to:
BRF, 15 The Chambers, Vineyard, Abingdon OX14 3FE

Service User Number: | 5 | 5 | 8 | 2 | 2 | 9 |

Name and full postal address of your bank or building society

To: The Manager	Bank/Building Society
Address	
	Postcode

Name(s) of account holder(s)

Branch sort code

| | | – | | | – | | | |

Bank/Building Society account number

| | | | | | | | | |

Reference number

| | | | | | | | | |

Instruction to your Bank/Building Society

Please pay The Bible Reading Fellowship Direct Debits from the account detailed in this instruction, subject to the safeguards assured by the Direct Debit Guarantee. I understand that this instruction may remain with The Bible Reading Fellowship and, if so, details will be passed electronically to my bank/building society.

Signature(s)

Banks and Building Societies may not accept Direct Debit instructions for some types of account.

Enabling all ages to grow in faith

Anna Chaplaincy
Living Faith
Messy Church
Parenting for Faith

The Bible Reading Fellowship (BRF) is a Christian charity that resources individuals and churches. Our vision is to enable people of all ages to grow in faith and understanding of the Bible and to see more people equipped to exercise their gifts in leadership and ministry.

To find out more about our work, visit

brf.org.uk